# What Leaders Say About *Versatility*

"Reading this book is a profound, in-your-face experience. It'll make you re-think the way you interact with others."
   **– Lorna D. Rolingson, PHR, Senior Director, Human Resources and Development, American Forest and Paper Association**

"Highly relevant to our business needs. I am in awe of her insights regarding our industry. Her workshops on this topic are just packed with tools people can use immediately. More importantly, she delivers in a way that's fun, which makes people retain and build on what she teaches. Be prepared: You're going to want to buy a copy of this book for everyone you care about."
   **– Thomas G. Bognanno, President and CEO, Community Health Charities**

"Condenses lessons that are tantamount to multiple careers in the nonprofit sector. Will become a well-worn reference in your library."
   **– Karen L. Hackett, FACHE, CAE, CEO, American Academy of Orthopedic Surgeons**

"Francie's message resonates. All who call ourselves leaders must gain and maintain this critical element of success: interpersonal versatility."
   **– Michael P. Hoagland, SPHR, CAE, Vice President, Human Resources, The American Institute of Architects**

"Interpersonal skills are essential to success in the nonprofit sector, both with your staff and members. Individuals who apply the learning in this book will experience greater personal success; organizations that integrate the principles Francie advocates will find it easier to attract and retain both talent and members."
   **– John M. Gray, President and Chief Executive Officer, Healthcare Distribution Management Association**

"Penetrating, masterful treatment of behavior that no one else is willing to be so up-front about."
   **– John Heberlein, Senior Director and Chief Financial Officer, The Endocrine Society**

"You're in for a real treat! Francie's book is as substantive, educational, and entertaining as her workshops and speeches!"
   **– Joe Ignacio, Director of Human Resources, American Physical Society**

"Francie Dalton has a talent for connecting with her audience immediately. They know she understands their perspective of the situation, whether it involves conflict management, supervision, negotiations, etc. That earned trust opens up opportunities for listening, reflecting, understanding, and most important, practicing these essential skill sets. Her engaging style and highly relevant, innovative workshops on interpersonal skills have been a valuable professional development tool for OSA's staff."

**– Liz Rogan, CEO, Optical Society of America**

"Francie Dalton knows how to make organizational retreats deliver transformative results, not just short-lived good feelings. Francie's work makes an exceptional, perhaps unique, contribution to cutting through the complexities of problem relationships that exist in most—if not all—membership organizations to increase cohesiveness and morale, boost productivity, and increase value."

**– Ernie Rosenberg, President and CEO, Soap and Detergent Association**

*"... an indispensable field manual for neutralizing even the most challenging workplace behaviors."*
—Red Cavaney, CAE, President and CEO, American Petroleum Institute

# Versatility

## How to Optimize Interactions When 7 Workplace Behaviors Are at Their Worst

# FRANCIE DALTON

asae & the center
for association leadership

WASHINGTON, D.C.

The author has worked diligently to ensure that all information in this book is accurate as of the time of publication and consistent with standards of good practice in the general management community. As research and practice advance, however, standards may change. For this reason it is recommended that readers evaluate the applicability of any recommendations in light of particular situations and changing standards.

The names used in the scenarios to demonstrate the behavioral styles were chosen randomly. Any similarities to actual events and individuals is strictly coincidental.

ASAE & The Center for Association Leadership
1575 I Street, NW
Washington, DC 20005-1103
Phone: (202) 626-2723; (888) 950-2723 outside the metropolitan Washington, DC area
Fax: (202) 220-6439
E-mail: books@asaecenter.org
We connect great ideas and great people to inspire leadership and achievement in the association community.

Keith C. Skillman, CAE, Vice President, Publications, ASAE & The Center for Association Leadership
Baron Williams, CAE, Director of Book Publishing, ASAE & The Center for Association Leadership

Cover design by Beth Lower, Art Director, ASAE & The Center for Association Leadership
Central cover image by Dan Austell
Interior design by Troy Scott Parker, CimarronDesign.com
Caricature ilustrations by Jason Shulman

This book is available at a special discount when ordered in bulk quantities. For information, contact the ASAE Member Service Center at (202) 371-0940.

A complete catalog of titles is available on the ASAE & The Center for Association Leadership website at www.asaecenter.org.

ISBN-13: 978-0-88034-300-8
ISBN-10: 0-88034-300-1

Printed in the United States of America.

10 9 8 7 6 5 4 3 2 1

# Contents

*For my clients,*
*who have the courage and tenacity to*
*slug it out every day in very tough arenas.*
*I am privileged to work with you.*

## SPECIAL THANKS

To Laura Jarrett, whose amazing versatility and business acumen stabilized both me and my company during the writing process. Her cheerful, unceasing, even selfless dedication and encouragement made this book— and so much more—possible.

To Marty Saggese, the Achiever who models that rare internal drive to consistently excel, and inspires those around him—including me—to strive to do the same. Perhaps it's alchemy, but what he catalyzes in others produces priceless, enduring, radial impacts.

To Chris Gray who, from the ripe old age of 16, has lent his energy and intellect to all that ultimately enabled this book.

To Kristy Hogbin and Nicole Teasley for their numerous, enthusiastic contributions to this book and all its permutations.


## ACKNOWLEDGEMENTS

To Keith Skillman, CAE, of ASAE & The Center for Association Leadership, who saw beyond a very rough first draft and gave this book the breath of life.

To Jason Shulman for his astonishing insights in creating the illustrations.

To Linda C. Chandler for her skillful editing of both content and structure.

# Foreword

I WAS FIRST INTRODUCED TO the content of this book when I attended a CEO Boot Camp sponsored by ASAE & The Center in San Diego. I was so intrigued by Francie Dalton's concepts about "The Chameleon's Edge" that I attended a longer session in Hawaii, and there I had a real epiphany about how I needed to approach my staff and board interactions.

Frankly, I think Francie's ideas rang true because they reflected so much of what I had learned in my life as a basketball player in high school and college, and her examples resonated with my experience specializing in sports marketing for Nike, Inc., and Converse, Inc. But when I moved into the CEO slot at the Women's Basketball Coaches Association in November 2001, I quickly recognized that I had not learned all I needed to know in the four years I'd already spent with the WBCA, even though I'd been preparing to assume the number-one position. I found myself thinking how little I knew about running a unique nonprofit association.

I have 28 board members, whose constituencies range from grassroots to professional; 14 full-time staff; and usually six or seven interns. That's a lot of people, and my daily interactions run the gamut of the behavioral types you'll learn about as you read this book.

I retained Francie as a consultant and have often called her for advice about how to handle board conflicts or issues with staff. She has become my "1-800-HELP" line! Much like a coach, Francie breaks down situations and the behaviors of the individuals involved, helping me discover what is behind the actions on the surface so that I can tailor my responses appropriately. As any association CEO knows, the process of communicating effectively with all the association's stakeholders sometimes can be exhausting, but the positive results can be exhilarating.

In associations, as in sports, some players on a team need quiet encouragement; some need a tough challenge; some need the promise of a tangible reward. Some you can command, and some you must persuade. A good coach figures out what makes every player tick and uses that knowledge to find each one's "sweet spot," to motivate each one individually, while bringing each person's strengths to focus on a team goal. In many cases a player's strengths can be like an Achilles' heel; a healthy spirit of competition can become a force that tears through others and refuses to compromise. An eye for detail can degenerate into a focus on minutia. The most creative game plan may lack good execution.

*Versatility: How to Optimize Interactions When 7 Workplace Behaviors Are at Their Worst* reminds you that versatility in your approach to others is the key. Francie notes the principal motivators and strengths as well as the decision-making mindset of seven behavioral styles you'll likely encounter in the workplace. She coaches you through giving them feedback appropriate to their styles. As you begin to recognize the strengths and weaknesses of the seven behavioral styles and practice Francie's tips about how to interact with them, you'll see your interactions become more effective and less frustrating, whether you're dealing with superiors or subordinates. The bottom line will be enhanced teamwork and consensus building.

And that couldn't be more important than now, when we are dealing with an increasingly diverse workforce. In our association, we've benefited greatly from the interns who work with us. The Millennials do a lot of reverse mentoring, teaching older staff about blogging, for instance. We've learned to allow for the fruit of the cross-pollination by becoming more versatile. Proficiency in working with workplace diversity makes us better able to succeed in the marketplace.

One of my most important jobs is to unify the staff, so when we come out onto the court of association business, we're a united team. There may be disagreement when we huddle, but my job is to be sure we will come out with one game plan—to win. My philosophy is to hire people who are stronger and better than me in certain areas so their skills will offset my weaknesses. We all recognize our roles as contributors. We are united and loyal. We have each other's back and one common mindset. That's the kind of unity you can achieve in your organization if you develop The Chameleon's Edge.

As Francie points out in the pages that follow, becoming versatile doesn't mean being less of who you are. It means becoming more of an Achiever, regardless of how you're wired. And whether you're a coach or an association executive, achievement is what we're all striving for. Have a great read!

   – Beth Bass, CEO
   Women's Basketball Coaches Association
   Atlanta

# Preface

L ET'S TAKE A FEW moments to assess whether including this book in your library will provide adequate, long-term utility. Consider these questions:

- Are you only rarely disappointed in or frustrated by the performance of others?
- Are you successful in getting polarized parties to collaborate effectively?
- Do you maintain your poise in adversarial situations?
- Are you able to neutralize acrimonious situations and individuals?

If so, then look for something else to read; you don't need this book. But if you're not satisfied with your answers to these questions, then this is your opportunity to gain immediate, significant enhancements in daily interactions with your business associates—without confrontation or pain—through expanded versatility.

In these pages you'll find real-world descriptions of the toughest-to-deal-with behaviors, with practical advice for how to optimize interacting with them. You'll see candid descriptions of behaviors we've all encountered, with no cosmetic enhancements, excuses, or justifications.

- The boss who's making you want to quit? In here.
- The subordinate who makes you crazy? In here.
- The peer who activates your gag reflex? Yep—in here.

Even the high-maintenance member, the perpetually hostile associate, and all the other irritating folks you just can't bring yourself to confront—they're all in here. You'll recognize them. And you'll also recognize yourself. You'll realize what you're doing that impedes your interpersonal success, and you'll learn specifically how to modify your approaches to be more effective.

Will I be stereotyping? You betcha! Absent prejudice, though, stereotyping has tremendous utility that cannot be debunked by emotionalism or the imputation of ill intent. Categorizing as used here isn't synonymous with permanent labeling, but is intended to portray patterns and provide guidelines to help you stabilize and optimize workplace interactions.

Will I be suggesting tactics that could be interpreted as manipulative? Absolutely! In fact, I've customized recommendations for each of the seven styles of behavior. Their purpose is not to puppeteer individuals but to accelerate the successful achievement of needed business results with less pain and stress for all parties involved.

Will either the stereotypes or manipulative recommendations be malicious? Nope, not a one. I'm not suggesting you expose, excoriate, or enable anyone. And I'm certainly not suggesting that you roll over for anyone. Instead, I'm recommending that you engage in a difficult, personally challenging undertaking, one that will be both diagnostic and remedial. Diagnostically, you'll make both extrospective and introspective assessments. Remedially, you'll apply deliberately selected bridge-building techniques to neutralize whatever ills currently exist in your professional interactions. By the time you reach the last chapter, you'll be equipped with seven benefits:

1. **The ability to predict the behavior of others.** Of course, I'm not suggesting you'll become clairvoyant, but you'll be equipped to recognize behavior patterns and to more accurately anticipate others' behavior, even if you don't know them well.

2. **Expanded versatility in your own behavioral repertoire.** Everyone has to interact with a variety of behaviors, some of which are considerably more challenging than others. You'll get lots of tips for how to diffuse the adversarial behavior of each of the seven styles.

3. **Increased effectiveness with others.** With an appreciation for the impact your behavior can have on others and the flexibility to alter your behavior to optimize interactions with others, you'll be better able to achieve desired results.

4. **Perspective that depersonalizes difficult interactions.** Your emotional and behavioral responses to what you see as the offending behaviors of others are determined in part by the degree to which you impute ill intent. By adjusting the lens through which you view the provocative actions of others, you can take the sting out of difficult interactions.

5. **A competitive advantage over others whose interpersonal skills are less well developed.** If you choose to apply the adapting techniques following the description of each style, your interpersonal competence will be visible to and discernable by others. Your behavior will distinguish you from most others, who will notice both the ease with which you neutralize even the most difficult behaviors, and your uncanny ability to access the discretionary energy of others.

6. **Higher self-esteem.** When you can look back on how you handled a difficult situation and feel good about your behavior, your self esteem increases. When you experience the benefit of editing yourself in real time rather than in hindsight, when you learn how to handle people and situations more successfully, you'll be proud of yourself more often, and this increases self-esteem. Those who consistently demonstrate behavior that is responsive instead of reactive enjoy high self-esteem—an outcome available to anyone who applies the advice contained in the following pages.

7. **More control over your vulnerabilities to others.** It's reasonable to assume that on more than one occasion, you've succumbed to the offensive actions of others. It's also reasonable to assume that you weren't proud of having lost your temper and composure. Instead of allowing others to get to you, push your buttons, and reduce you to your lower self, you can use this book to learn how to maintain poise and professionalism, even when the behaviors of others are inflammatory. You can manage your vulnerability to others by better understanding what evokes your own worst behavior, and by using techniques that help you maintain equanimity and effectiveness, whether the provocateur is your superior or your subordinate.

Of course, securing these benefits presumes that you apply the requisite self-discipline. And it will take discipline. As with most of the other professional development initiatives you've tackled, the recommendations you'll discover in these pages won't be intuitive, comfortable, or easy. But before you sigh in exasperation at yet another book that suggests you shoulder an additional developmental burden requiring still more discipline, consider a different perspective on the concept of self-discipline.

If you agree that interpersonal effectiveness is indeed key to your success in business, then set aside the punishing, sacrificing, suffering connotations typically associated with the term *self-discipline* and adopt a more palliative perspective. The Latin origin of both "discipline" and "disciple" is *discipulus,* meaning "one who learns." Arguably, when you set your sights on any desired outcome, you become a student of that which will assure success. Whatever struggles you face as you move toward improving your workplace interactions, decide to persevere from a posture of learning, not as an exercise in self-discipline but as an act of discipleship to that which will, indisputably, enhance your success.

My hope is that this book helps you achieve and maintain awareness of the link between your behavior and that of others, that it inspires you to choose to behave in ways that elicit the business results you need, and that it instills within you esteem for the use of behavior as the powerful tool it is.

*Francie*

Francie Dalton

# Versatility as the Essential Competence

ONLY RECENTLY HAVE THE long-simmering changes in the composition and characteristics of the United States workforce become so pervasive as to demand employer response. With broad implications for organizational America and for the nonprofit sector specifically, coping successfully with these changes will elevate the function of management to a veritable art form. Paramount among the managerial competencies required is versatility.

## Versatility and the Imminent Workforce Crisis

No matter what source you choose—Department of Labor, Bureau of Labor Statistics, Department of Commerce—the forecast is the same for the United States:

- By 2010, there'll be 10 million more jobs than workers.
- By 2013, there'll be a shortage of 6 million degreed workers.
- By 2020, the shortage of workers will be 14 million.

And these numbers are net of the talent we import and the jobs we export!

The implications of these shortages for the nonprofit sector are numerous and serious. First, the competition for workers will be intense. Nonprofits can anticipate that losing good employees will be a constant problem and that a 30 percent annual turnover rate will be comparatively low.

Second, in addition to a quantitative deficit, a qualitative deficit is imminent. The United States currently ranks seventh among the world's 30 most industrialized nations in producing college graduates in the 25- to 34-year-old age group. This exacerbates the coming shortage of more than six million degreed workers, threatening organizational ability to sustain both the pace of project execution and the volume of valued services.

Third, these projections reveal a significant and tough-to-manage gap in the ages of workers. Our workforce will include those under 30 and over 49, but comparatively few workers who are age 30 to 49. Managerial talent will have to be sufficient to manage each group effectively and have the skills needed to ensure that all the groups work together productively.

Fourth, as technological advances continue to allow the automation of physical and technical jobs, remaining positions will increasingly require the high-touch style of management traditionally attributed to females. Current and aspiring male executives will have to achieve fluency with a relationship-based style of management to compete successfully with women.

Don't be deceived into thinking that the economic slump current as of this writing will negate these projections. At best, market conditions will merely delay this forecast a year or two. Indeed, well-informed business leaders are already aware that retention is now a top strategic priority. As your organization engages in the highly competitive endeavor to retain talent, success will be determined by whether you can offer alignment to existing and potential employees in three workplace arenas: (1) between job content and the developmental aspirations of individuals, (2) between work environment and the needs or preferences of individuals, and (3) between managerial style and the needs of a diverse work force.

## Aligning Job Content and Individual Aspirations

Job content is typically expressed in some combination of position description and specific outcomes discrete to a given review period. Usually the position description isn't negotiable and no effort is made to customize the job duties to the specific interests of the employee. Further, although someone can be promoted into or out of a position, the job of the hiring manager has always been to find a candidate who, for the foreseeable future, wants the position as described. Today, retaining employees means being willing to revise and reformat positions, to mix and match duties, to clarify from day one the path from one's initial position to one's desired position. This challenge requires ongoing, substantive communication with employees and applicants, integrating their input into both the design of new positions and the redesign of existing positions.

Although it isn't realistic to let employees design their own jobs, it is possible to be more flexible about who does what. True, there will always be specific functions that must be performed, and yes, most of us will always have to shoulder some complement of less than delightful duties, but giving employees more control over a significant portion of their job content will make the difference between attracting or keeping them and losing them. Consider the following.

**For existing positions:** (1) Allow collaboration among groups of employees to determine how to enhance the work products of one another, help one another grow, and enrich the overall organization. (2) Allow administrative support personnel to review a comprehensive list of all the duties required for all such positions, and let them divide the responsibilities consistent with their preferences, ensuring that each has growth opportunities and a fair share of the more mundane functions.

**For new positions:** (1) Allow candidates who have interest or experience in two different openings to work a week or two in each job to determine which they prefer. (2) If you have a candidate, for example, who is qualified for a job in your accounting department but whose real interest is in your legal department, consider collaborating with the managers in both departments to structure the position so that some mix of work becomes reasonable and useful.

Sound impractical? Are you thinking that you can't hold multiple job openings hostage for weeks while a candidate makes a choice between the positions? Are you assuming that managers in different departments won't be willing to restructure jobs to accommodate candidates' interests? Think again. Economists are predicting a shortage of six million degreed individuals by 2016. Organizations will be turning somersaults to get and keep employees.

## Aligning Work Environment With Individual Preferences

You'll be ahead of the game if you recognize now the need to offer a smorgasbord of options within the work environment to align with individual preferences. The more of the following benefits your organization can offer, the better positioned you'll be to attract and retain talent.

- **Work hours:** 35-hour work weeks, flex-time, job sharing, sabbaticals
- **Work place:** telecommuting, employer-supplied home offices
- **Education:** full tuition reimbursement, mentoring, coaching, corporate universities, and certification programs
- **Professional services:** legal, mortgage, and other financial services
- **Personal services:** concierge and personal assistant services, temporary/emergency/back-up transportation to/from work
- **Family services:** on-site or paid day care for children, after school programs, elder care

- **Facilities:** on-site or paid gym, health and recreational facilities, food services, personalized work stations
- **Retirement benefits:** phased retirement plans, access to long-term care insurance
- **Leave:** maternity and paternity leave, five weeks vacation from first year of employment
- **Technology:** state-of-the-art equipment, convenience-enabling devices for professional and personal use

## Aligning Managerial Style With the Needs of a Diverse Workforce

All this collaboration and customization will necessitate considerable managerial skills, which are achieved in one of two ways: at the dear price of long-term experience or with a substantial and ongoing investment in professional development and training. Increasingly frequent merger and acquisition activity in the corporate arena has reduced the number of dues-paying members and donor organizations, requiring budget cuts by nonprofits. The result? Management training—indeed, any training—is often viewed as an unaffordable luxury.

As your organization struggles to disperse scarce financial resources across competing needs, consider three facts about management training: (1) strategic initiatives cannot be achieved without a sufficient number of staff who are at least adequately competent; (2) an expert level of management will be required to navigate the looming workforce crisis; therefore, (3) how you prioritize and fund management training will determine your survival.

Unless and until senior management exerts the same level of scrutiny on the management function as is already applied to the functions of membership and finance, the impact of poor management on retention will be impossible to mitigate. The one-style-of-management-fits-all approach must be shed in favor of a comprehensive template of highly developed interpersonal skills including:

- Versatility in communicating effectively with numerous behavior styles, cultures, and skill levels

- The ability to engage, motivate, and appreciate employees not just en masse, but as individuals, ensuring employees know they are valued

- The ability to synthesize seemingly disparate preferences, needs, and opportunities into a blended composite that serves both macro- and micro-level objectives

Make no mistake. Serious retention initiatives aren't going to be optional. That you may demean all this as over-coddling or pampering does not make it any less true. Whether you believe it or not, high salaries and interesting work won't be enough to retain employees. You can ignore this advice until the marketplace makes it indisputably clear, by which time your proactive competitors will have snagged all the best people, or you can act now, ensuring that your organization has set the retention standard in your industry.

## Versatility in the Nonprofit Sector

When compared to their counterparts in the for-profit arena, nonprofit employees exhibit certain traits that seem disproportionately resident within associations, foundations, and charities, regardless of hierarchy or function.

Generally, nonprofit employees are cause driven. Fundamentally attracted by the mission of their organizations, they are proud to be associated with a cause, are committed to the goals, and care very much about deploying their skills in ways that benefit society at large. In particular, Generations X and Y want to be associated with "standing for something" and need to see organizational behavior that demonstrates social responsibility and global citizenship. Within this subset of the population, family and social responsibility have become more attractive than personal enrichment, with compensation being subordinated to those values.

Correlated to a cause-driven orientation can be a kind individual nature that makes it hard for many managers in the nonprofit arena to confront poor performers or other problem employees. Preferring to maintain workplace friendships and avoid unpleasantness, nonprofit managers tend to ignore ugly truths and tolerate performance issues, even when others lodge repeated complaints. In the absence of consequences for poor performance and/or disruptive behavior, numerous negative impacts are perpetuated throughout the organization.

Because they deal daily with polarized factions within their membership and on their committees, nonprofit employees have mastered the skill of equivocation. Indeed, so sophisticated is their ability to hedge that a clear choice, an explicit decision, even an unambiguous opinion can be an anomaly. Discerning the actual message from tact-laden conversations can bring decision making and problem solving to a grinding halt.

Nonprofit employees often demonstrate a level of emotional maturity that can be considerably lower than that of their for-profit counterparts. Several factors are contributory. (1) Employees who have never worked in the for-profit sector mistakenly believe that the extremely generous benefits provided by their nonprofit employers are standard. (2) For many nonprofit employees, it's not uncommon for their organization to be their only employer since entering the workforce. Coupled with their manager's reluctance to give even constructive criticism, (3) these employees often exhibit what those with more diverse work experience see as a sense of entitlement.

Although it's true that the membership orientation, reliance on volunteers, and the committee structure embedded within nonprofit operations can sometimes trump business acumen, impede efficacy, and even discourage robust discussion, these operational mores are too often blamed for what is, in fact, an excessively deferential culture. Nonprofit employees frequently claim to be victimized by member whim, helpless to influence their committees, when the truth is that they themselves are conflict averse and unwilling to disagree with their stakeholders. It is standard operating procedure in some nonprofits for acquiescence to masquerade as oppression, particularly when management views anything other than complete submission to be anathema. A frequent outcome of such subservience is the blanket acceptance of member-requested new or expanded initiatives without negotiating corresponding increases in resources, without shedding or reshuffling existing priorities, and without advocacy on behalf of staff. When management fails to aggressively maintain a balance between initiatives and resources, the turnover that results from unreasonable workloads exacerbates tensions even further.

Another oft-bemoaned descriptor of nonprofit organizations is that consensus decision making can become synonymous with no decision making. Progress can be thwarted, even suffocated, when frankness is hijacked by a too collaborative work style or an aversion to constructive conflict. Assuredly, consensus building is essential to the business of nonprofits; but when used as a proxy for decision making, when used to cloak an inability to constructively confront issues, it renders managers ineffective. Rebounding from an established pattern of this behavior is virtually impossible. A suspended state of inaction perpetuated by indecisiveness under the guise of consensus building is an indication of one's interpersonal incompetence—not one's graciousness, patience, benevolence, or political acumen.

With the exception of academia, in no other organizational structure are silos more prevalent than in nonprofits. Increasingly severe budget constraints have instigated the need to do much more, much faster, with much less. Already inundated with volunteer, member, and Hill meetings, employees are loathe to devote precious time attending internal meetings for superficially collaborative purposes. Mid-year imposition of additional expectations on frequently under-staffed departments means there just isn't time for the luxury of cross-training. Because the competition for additional resource allocations among highly accountable business units is intense, justifications for new positions have to be unassailable, and to be so, they must identify discrete competencies. Because staffs are often necessarily composed of subject matter experts, there is little toler-ance for other internal perspectives that are only peripherally relevant to one's core responsibilities. Such business environments foster cut-throat territorialism, not teamwork.

As nonprofit employers strive to improve workplace interactions, generic courses in the interpersonal skills genre are inadequate. Equally inapplicable, at least for most nonprofits, is an academic or scientific approach to relation-ship management. Further still, neither long tenure nor residence in the C-Suite is sufficient to steward others' developmental needs in the interpersonal arena. Instead, what's needed is a set of well structured templates, rich in examples that resonate, and grounded in practical application to the day-to-day work life of nonprofit employees.

Focused on increasing your effectiveness with all your work-related stake-holders, this book provides a detailed, contextually relevant representation of seven behavioral styles you likely encounter on a daily basis. Peppered with blended but true stories of actual occurrences in nonprofit organizations, the advice offered here has been fire tested in settings just like yours. If you're striving to fast track enhancements to your relational effectiveness, this book will help you develop the requisite personal versatility and by so doing will help you gain exceptional visibility. You'll not only increase the ease with which you succeed, you'll also increase the frequency with which you emerge as flameproof, even from high stakes venues. (OK…OK…maybe you'll still be a little singed around the edges—but, hey—that's a lot better than toasted!)

# CHAPTER 1

# Gaining Versatility: The Underpinnings

YOU CAN BE A master tactician, with no one to serve; a brilliant strategist, with no one to lead. You can be loaded with talent and still be passed over for promotion or bursting with business acumen without ever experiencing success. You can even be absolutely right about an issue and still fail to prevail. You can allow the resulting disappointment and frustration to fuel debilitating resentment that festers for the rest of your career, or you can begin to examine your role in the outcomes you've experienced to date and recognize that you had a lot more control over those outcomes than you realized. Talent and brains just aren't enough to ensure success; in fact, they're not even prerequisites. What is a prerequisite, indeed essential, for sustained success, is personal versatility—the ability to optimize interactions even when others are at their worst. That's what the workshop "The Chameleon's Edge" is all about: learning to package what you want from others in a way that makes them want to give it to you.

Attendee behavior in hundreds of workshops over the past 18 years makes it reasonable to predict that you'll scan this book to read about the behavioral styles you find most annoying. Although you'll likely find your opinions of your nemeses validated, the recommendations for improving the relationships won't resonate and may rankle—at least initially—because all the advice refers to what YOU can do to neutralize antipathy.

Like most workshop attendees, you won't likely want to be the one to change, the one who, as usual, has to take the high road. In the words of one association executive: "I don't have a problem adapting to most styles; I can deal with them smooth as silk. But with others, when I try to modify my behavior to work with them, it's like climbing up a hill with molasses on it. It's just really difficult. It makes my guts churn, and I get stressed. I don't enjoy it. And no matter how clear it is that I'm making an effort, they don't reciprocate."

Against the daily grind of such realities, getting yourself to the point where you're willing to apply the suggestions in this book may be particularly difficult. But with the contextual grounding provided in this chapter, you can begin to develop a preliminary receptivity toward expanding your personal versatility—the essential competence for attaining The Chameleon's Edge.

## 10 Guiding Principles

These 10 principles are the framework for all that follows. They also have implications for almost every facet of business: revitalizing talent, constructing high performance teams, easing reporting relationships, enhancing the function of committee staffing, optimizing the performance review process, motivating individual performance, even making operational units more efficacious.

### Principle 1: You Can't Change Others.

Although some people may have power over others in the form of performance ratings, raises, bonuses, or new opportunities, the use of such power won't change others' behavior absent their desire to do so. At worst, the overt use of power inflames active resistance and at best, elicits mere compliance. Even if you could impose extreme measures to provoke behavior change, any such change would be inauthentic and would not be sustained over time.

Fundamentally, human behavior is the result of three equally weighted components: basic needs, personal beliefs, and the current situation. If you're the boss, you may be able to control a current situation, but you can't control someone else's needs or beliefs. If you're anyone other than the boss—and perhaps even if you are—at most, you have only a 33 percent chance of controlling someone's behavior. Not great odds. So if you're waiting for others to change because you think they should change, you may as well wait for pigs to fly.

What you can control is the degree to which you choose to adapt. Without suppressing who you really are, without turning yourself inside out and becoming a fake, you can become more versatile. Purposely managing your interactions with others will be considerably easier if you do so using their language. To some extent, you're already doing this. Don't you already modify your word choice, your tone, even your physiology, depending on whether you're communicating with your boss, a member, your subordinate, a vendor, or a confidant? Here's the essence of this principle: You have more control over the outcomes of your interactions than you might think; it's just that the path leading to increased control may be counterintuitive—and galling.

Consider this: Even if you're absolutely right that your nemesis should be the one to change, the method you employ to elicit that change may be absolutely wrong. As long as you're expecting the other person to change, you've surrendered control of the situation. You can inspire people to change their behavior, but you cannot make them do so. Instead of fighting the fact that you can't convince others to change their behavior to align with your preferences, get busy adapting your own! People are successful in coping with the difficult behavior of others because they change their own behavior, not to become like the other person but to better manage the outcome of the interaction. Instead of trying to change others, learn to adapt your own style so that the other person actually wants to play nice in the sandbox.

## Principle 2: Understanding Each Behavioral Style Is Essential.

Strong emotional resistance to understanding others' behavior isn't unusual. A little probing often reveals the misconception that understanding is a code word for touchy-feely stuff and that the pursuit of understanding is tantamount to capitulation. Not so. As any married couple will attest, it is possible to vehemently disagree with your spouse while simultaneously understanding his or her position. Understanding isn't synonymous with agreement; it's a tactic in the negotiation of agreements.

Still others see understanding as that which enables them to tolerate, ignore, work around, prevail over, or silence another. Again, not so. Instead, understanding your adversary's perspectives and motives equips you to identify more options for resolving discord and establishing partnerships. Being able to discern behavioral styles that are needed in a particular situation, learning how to recognize those styles when you see them, and having the wisdom to include those folks appropriately will accelerate the success of difficult interactions. Understanding, then, is a state of cognitive clarity that facilitates the development and execution of an effective plan for working together successfully.

## Principle 3: Packaging for Success Is a Skill You Can Learn.

If you're frustrated in your efforts to optimize interactions with others, chances are at least one of the causal factors is the way you package your message. Those who are successful in coping with difficult people know how to package what they want from others in a way that makes others want to give it to them. This isn't bribery, and it doesn't exploit others. True, it is manipulation, but it's benign manipulation—without malice—deployed solely to enable the achievement of business results without unnecessary rancor.

Some people resent the very idea that packaging techniques should have to be used at all. Others chafe at the hyperbolized assumption that interpersonal success will be elusive unless an endless number of packaging techniques have been mastered. But expecting someone else to change just because it's your opinion that they should isn't usually sufficient to compel the desired change. Simply telling a micromanager, for example, to stop micromanaging isn't likely to be effective; demanding that a belligerent bully demonstrate sincere compassion isn't likely to produce the desired result.

Instead, there are ways to wrap what you need from others in packaging that magnifies its appeal to each style. The techniques aren't rocket science, and they aren't difficult to use except to the extent that one's attitude about them can make their use difficult. What reticence there is to the use of these techniques bodes well for the motivated reader, since only a small minority of people seem to use them and doing so makes clearly visible an unusual fluency in working effectively even with the most difficult people. Remember: The purpose of using adapting techniques is to optimize interactions. Resentment or contempt for the use of packaging techniques is effective only in preventing improvement in your relationships. You can choose not to use them, and you'll continue to get the results you're already getting, or you can use them and enjoy an immediate reduction in the severity and frequency of stress in your interactions. Packaging eases and accelerates interpersonal success—which eases and accelerates everything!

## Principle 4: Behavior Is a Method, Not an Outcome.

If you focus on and react to others' behavior, you'll likely exacerbate your difficulties. If, instead, you recognize behavior as a tool that's being used to acquire a specific outcome, you'll be much better equipped to identify options for reducing acrimony.

Try applying this principle to your advantage in daily life. Think of an instance when someone's behavior irritated you. What was the irritating behavior? Now think about what the behavior was being used to achieve. For example, if the behavior was intimidation, perhaps the desired result was to frighten someone into submission. If you recognize that the intimidating behavior is being deployed as a device to prevail in an argument, it's easier to ignore the behavior and stay focused on the substantive components of the argument. Suppose the irritating behavior was constant interruption so that you could never finish a sentence. Consider the utility of being able to distinguish among at least three possible reasons why the interruptions occurred: (a) to establish intellectual superiority, (b) to demonstrate thinking in alignment with your own, or (c) to give voice to unbridled enthusiasm. It's unlikely you'd handle all three scenarios the same way.

Discerning the desired outcome of others' behavior is crucial to successfully navigating difficult interactions. Choose to focus on desired outcomes rather than on behaviors. The former will reveal options, increasing the likelihood of faster, easier resolution. The latter will merely prove inflammatory, increasing the likelihood of an impasse.

## Principle 5: Imputing Ill Intent Exacerbates Tension.

Although certainly there are exceptions, folks don't usually set out on a deliberate mission to upset others with their behavior; instead, they are just behaving in a way that is consistent with their wiring. The impact of their behavior on you may well be negative, but it doesn't necessarily follow that the negative impact was intentional. In highly charged conflicts, the parties often assume each is being deliberately obstinate when, in fact, neither party is even aware of having created that perception. When you assume another's behavior is intentionally designed to provoke, you expand the dimensions of the problem beyond the confines of business issues and into the arena of emotion. In consequence, you're more likely to take it personally, further taxing your self-control and increasing your vulnerability to behaving in ways you won't be proud of later. The imputation of ill intent can be incendiary and serves no constructive purpose. Persisting in this practice calls into question your own intentions.

## Principle 6: Consider the Flip Side.

Here's a tough question for you. Can you identify one behavior of your own that you know others find aggravating? Now honestly, don't you consider their aggravation invalid? Don't you believe that if they simply had the right perspective, they would realize your behavior is not only appropriate but exactly what's needed? A single behavior can be viewed in dramatically different ways by different people. Try thinking of this as two sides of the same coin. People naturally tend to deem justifiable those behaviors they esteem and deem unjustifiable the behaviors they disesteem.

Here's another example. If you value assertiveness as a behavioral characteristic that produces success, you may be surprised to learn that others can see you as aggressive—or worse—as a bully. Aghast and dismayed though you may be to learn of this, your bewilderment doesn't nullify their perceptions. Your knowledge of your true intentions can blind you to your actual effect on others. Your intentions notwithstanding, what you view to be an appropriate application of your positive traits can be experienced by others as if amplified exponentially.

We don't get to choose how we're wired, but we do get to choose the intensity with which we deploy our behavioral characteristics. Now that you're aware of the potential for dissonance in how your behaviors may be experienced by others, hold yourself to a higher standard. Look for subtle indications that you're coming on too strong or too soft and make the adjustment necessary to optimize your interactions.

Just as you don't want your behavior to be misinterpreted or wrongly exaggerated in the minds of others, so must you guard against succumbing to misinterpreting others' behavior. If you wish that others would look past what feels to them like bullying and see only the benign assertiveness that you intended, you must be equally poised to reciprocate. Look for the flip side, for the strength that underlies what you perceive to be another's weakness, and give him or her the benefit of the doubt.

### Principle 7: It's Not About How You Feel.
During the time you're at work, whether at the office or on the convention floor, at a board or committee meeting, on the phone or on a plane, your behavior is being rented by your employer. The rental payment flows to you in the form of salary and benefits, in exchange for which you're expected to behave in ways that secure targeted business results. Instead, what often happens is that employees indulge in the luxury of behaving the way they feel, even when doing so impedes the work plan. In badly snarled relationships, it's often not the intricacies of the business issues but the emotions of the parties involved that form the barrier to resolution.

Two-year-olds get to have tantrums. Adolescents get to have meltdowns. When salaried professionals engage in emotionally volatile or immature behavior, it reflects badly on both the individual and the organization. Claiming that behavior contrary to your real feelings renders you inauthentic, fake, or plastic is just a weak excuse for choosing not to edit yourself appropriately. What resonates with and catches the attention of those with the power to promote you is behavior that is poised and professional, even amid the provocative actions of others.

Even if your self-control is well honed, the urge to let loose and vent pent-up emotions can sometimes become irresistible. So the next time you see someone surrender to that need, set aside righteous indignation in favor of graciousness. Assume that the deficiency in versatility you're witnessing is based on a lack of knowledge about easy-to-deploy behavioral alternatives. Share this book with them. Help them build their self-esteem and their careers. Help them discover the options they need to be effective regardless of the provocations they encounter. Most importantly, model behavior that demonstrates the ability to subordinate what feels good to the acquisition of desired results.

## Principle 8: One Size Does Not Fit All.

Ignore reality for just a moment, and imagine that a big, strapping, lumberjack-type union employee named Boris has been dispatched to the exhibit floor to help construct your booth. Your display is particularly labor intensive and is assigned a space farthest from the engineer's shop. Even before your crates were on site, you knew construction of your booth would involve multiple trips up and down the full length of the exhibit hall by union laborers. To your astonishment, Boris shows up at your booth wearing (well, sort of wearing) candy-apple red stiletto heels obviously sized for a petite individual. If you were concerned before about the quality of customer service you could reasonably expect given the complexity and location of your booth, those concerns have just ballooned. Overcome with empathy, you inquire about Boris' comfort and learn that he has been prohibited from removing the shoes. How energetic is Boris? How's his productivity? What about his attitude? How service oriented is he? Is he motivated to help you?

Here's the point. As ridiculous as this story may be, it's no more ridiculous than expecting your preferred behavior style to suit everyone. Just as not everyone wears the same shoe size, interpersonal effectiveness can't be attained using a one-size-fits-all approach.

To the extent that you're experiencing a lack of interpersonal success, a likely contributing factor is the expectation that others accommodate and adapt to your behavior style. Placing a premium on your own behavioral comfort zone and expecting your professional associates to treat you as if your behavior is the baseline to which all other behaviors must be adjusted is as unrealistic as Boris in stilettos.

Remember, in an increasingly diverse workforce, retention and, therefore, success will depend on the ability to discern and provide resonant management. Having sufficient personal versatility to quickly tailor your style of interaction to each individual is the secret to interpersonal success.

## Principle 9: Focus on the Four P's.

Think of all the opportunities you've had to observe behavior throughout your work day. Think of those who work in close proximity to you: those with whom you work on projects, fellow team members, and internal customers. Start paying attention to their behavior. Before long, you'll be able to discern patterns. Once you identify patterns of behavior, the likelihood that you can accurately predict others' behavior in similar future circumstances increases. As soon as their behavior becomes predictable, you can use the packaging techniques provided at the end of each chapter to optimize each interaction. Although certainly no one adheres to a single pattern 100 percent of the time, even incremental gains in your interpersonal effectiveness can net huge dividends. So **P**ay attention to others' behavior; identify **P**atterns in their behavior; **P**redict others' behavior as you prepare to interact with them, and then **P**ackage your own behavior accordingly.

## Principle 10: Alignment ≠ Confinement.

If you know your strengths aren't compatible with the function you're performing, if too frequent adaptations are required for effectiveness with too many people, then work toward releasing yourself from such confinement. Instead, strive to achieve alignment between your strengths and your functions. Commit to deploying yourself within contexts that showcase your competencies and de-emphasize your weaknesses. Decide on a professional pursuit that features your strengths. You have more flexibility to do this than you may realize. What are you doing when your strengths are shining? Where are your strengths needed? What business pursuits are your strengths ideally suited to expand or enhance? How can you help others do this? And by the way, what are you waiting for?

FIGURE 1
## THE HEPTAGON OF BEHAVIORAL STYLES

## The Heptagon of Behavioral Styles

Why, you may well ask, is a heptagon being used in Figure 1 when eight different styles are depicted? Why not an octagon? Here's the answer. Appearing in the center of the heptagon to indicate that it is not separate from but resident within all seven behavior styles, the Achiever helps you manifest only the best of your template of styles. Between the Achiever and any of the seven styles there are no barriers or impediments except those of your own making, so the degree to which the Achiever dominates your behavior is a matter of deliberate choice.

For all seven styles in Figure 1, you'll learn:

1. How to recognize them
2. Their strengths
3. Their greatest needs
4. How they make decisions
5. Their reaction to feedback and how best to provide it
6. How to manage your vulnerability to each style as your boss
7. Adapting to each style as your boss
8. How to manage your vulnerability to each style as your subordinate
9. Adapting to each style as your subordinate

You will also find actual, sanitized 360-degree inputs from their superiors, peers, and subordinates.

Although each behavioral style will be presented in the following chapters as if it were a distinct and discrete style, in reality everyone is a blend of styles. Most people use at least three styles regularly. Even though some of your associates might seem to fit a particular profile exactly, it's highly unlikely that you've encountered any single style in its pure form. Once you've acquired a solid understanding of the seven behavioral styles, you'll be ready to learn in Chapter 9 how the Achiever can positively influence every style, increase your versatility, and help you attain The Chameleon's Edge.

Sections 6 through 9 on the preceding page are not relevant to Achievers and will not appear in Chapter 9. Special sections unique to Achievers will be included instead. Additionally, adapting techniques are specific to superiors and subordinates. Because peer behavior is some blend of that displayed by superiors or subordinates, readers must discern what subset of the tips provided will be effective with peers.

Rather than focusing on what makes each style wonderful, this book is devoted to what makes each style particularly difficult. A serious handling of behavior as the single most divisive force in the workplace requires a disproportionate concentration on what's most challenging about each style, so be prepared for the descriptions to seem excessively harsh. The seven behaviors will be treated as though they were discrete rather than the blended styles they actually are. In consequence, the rough edges of each style will seem hyperbolized, dramatized, and emotionalized.

Believe it or not, of the seven behavioral styles yours is the one that's most difficult for someone else. So put on your seatbelt; the treatment of your dominant style will be no less merciless than for any other and the impacts of your behaviors will be no more shrouded in or mitigated by your positive characteristics than that of any other style.

Nonprofit employees are especially aware that they accomplish a greater volume of work with less stress when they're able to collaborate effectively with others. Cognitive awareness, however, is insufficient at the moment when another's behavior is most repugnant. You need explicit, simple tips that you can implement even when your patience is being sorely tried. The purpose of this book is to equip you to interact successfully at those very moments.

Even though there's no cookie cutter approach for consistent effectiveness with others' behavior, this book is as clear a roadmap as you're ever going to get for optimizing your workplace interactions so you can secure the business results you need without the stress-inducing energy drain you may be experiencing now.

## Customizing Your Context for Learning

The following three sections are offered to personalize your learning experience, enhancing the value and utility of this book to your specific circumstances. Thoughtful reflection in completing each section will significantly enhance your return on the investment you make in reading this book.

### A. Benchmarking Your Workplace Relationships

Once you've completed the notations requested in this section, set your work aside until the scoring process is described in Chapter 10. Trust that you'll gain considerable benefits, and maybe even some real surprises, if you comply with this instruction.

- **A.1:** Identify at least three individuals at work whose behavior you find especially irritating. Jot down their names, along with the most irritating behaviors displayed by each.

- **A.2:** Identify at least three individuals who are particularly easy for you to collaborate with at work. Jot down their names, along with the behaviors that make interactions with them so effortless.

- **A.3:** Identify at least one person at work who has been an inspiration to you; someone to whom you would turn for advice, whose behavior you admire and aspire to emulate. Briefly describe this individual's behavior.

### B. Self-Assessment Mechanism

On page 13 is a Self-Assessment Mechanism, Figure 2. Complete the assessment by indicating the degree to which you possess each of the listed traits, assigning a minimum score of 1 for characteristics that are least like you, and a maximum score of 5 for characteristics that are most like you. Strive to avoid assigning the more ambivalent rating of 3. Once you've made your selections, it's important that you do not change your answers. Later in the book, you'll be given a URL where you can type in these answers and receive a computer-generated set of scores.

### C. The Predictive Grid

The Predictive Grid (Figure 3) has been designed to enable a comparative analysis between the scores you assign yourself before learning about the behavioral styles, and the scores you assign yourself after learning about each style. As you read the next eight chapters, consider how closely your workplace behavior aligns with the descriptions. When you see the notation in each chapter that asks you to do so, enter a number from 5 to 25 in Column B of The Predictive Grid, indicating to what extent you believe your workplace behavior reflects that style. Additional instructions for the use of The Predictive Grid appear in Chapter 10.

FIGURE 2
## SELF-ASSESSMENT MECHANISM

| Characteristic | Your Score |
|---|---|
| ABRUPT | |
| AFRAID OF FAILURE | |
| ANGRY | |
| AVOID FINALIZING THINGS | |
| "BOTTOM LINE" ORIENTED | |
| COMPASSIONATE | |
| CONTROLLING | |
| CYNICAL | |
| DETAIL ORIENTED | |
| DISORGANIZED | |
| DOUBLE/TRIPLE CHECK THINGS | |
| ENJOY SELF | |
| ENJOY THE SPOTLIGHT | |
| FAST RATE OF SPEECH | |
| FEAR OF RISK | |
| FLASHY | |
| FREE-SPIRITED | |
| GROUCHY | |
| HAPPY | |
| IMAGINATIVE | |
| IMPULSIVE | |
| INTIMIDATING | |
| JOVIAL | |
| LAID BACK | |
| NEED EVERYONE TO AGREE | |
| PEACEFUL | |
| PERFECTIONIST | |
| PLEASANT DISPOSITION | |
| PRECISE | |
| "PROCESS" ORIENTED | |
| REASSURING TO OTHERS | |
| RESERVED | |
| SELF FULFILLED | |
| PERPETUAL SENSE OF URGENCY | |
| SERENE | |
| SUBMISSIVE | |
| SUPERIOR | |
| USE LOTS OF CLICHES | |
| USUALLY IN A HURRY | |
| WORRIER | |

*This page is intentionally left blank*

# THE PREDICTIVE GRID

| A | B | C | D |
|---|---|---|---|
| Behavioral Style | As you read each of the "style" chapters, indicate your anticipated score (must ≥ 5 and ≤ 25) | Enter your computer-generated score here. *Do this only after completing the book!* You'll be given the URL later | Enter your Personalized Action Plan based on differences between B and C |
| Commander | | | |
| Drifter | | | |
| Attacker | | | |
| Pleaser | | | |
| Performer | | | |
| Avoider | | | |
| Analytical | | | |
| Achiever | | | |

# CHAPTER 2

# The Commander

**DESCRIPTORS**

| | |
|---|---|
| SUCCINCT, ABRUPT | DISTANT, ALOOF, NOT WARM |
| CONSERVATIVE DRESS | RARELY GIVES PRAISE |
| DOMINEERING, CONTROLLING | RESULTS ORIENTED |
| HIGHLY STRUCTURED | CONFIDENT |
| NOT INTROSPECTIVE | CONSISTENT |
| POOR DELEGATOR | DEMANDS PERFECTION |
| WON'T BE QUESTIONED | DECISIVE |
| RESISTS INNOVATION | INSPIRES CONFIDENCE |
| SOLID EYE CONTACT | SENSE OF URGENCY |
| ERECT POSTURE | EXUDES POWER |
| NOT MALICIOUS | FAIR |

*C*ONSIDER JOE, A DEPUTY EXECUTIVE DIRECTOR. *Well known to be an extreme micromanager, he needs to control every decision, no matter how minor. Even business conversations among staff are discouraged. When board members visit the organization, they are personally escorted at all times by Joe, ensuring no unsupervised contact with staff. Because all decisions are made exclusively by Joe, there is never sufficient time to communicate the decisions to those affected, generating a tremendous volume of rework and retarding productivity. In addition to impeding obviously and easily available efficacies, Joe's management style chokes off innovation. Staff have taken the initiative to produce plans for achieving specific instructions from member committees regarding website functionality, publication improvements, and leadership enhancements, but none have been implemented. Their recommendations are perpetually stuck in the sieve of executive review.*

Joe's style of management typifies Commander behavior. Natural leaders who are comfortable making even high-risk decisions, Commanders can be demanding and domineering. They take control effortlessly, as if telling others what to do were their destiny. More comfortable with work than emotions, Commanders are aggravated by phrases such as "I feel," "Let's share," or "maybe." Economical with words and naturally aloof toward others, Commanders are crisp and direct to the point of abruptness and consider tact an unnecessary waste of time.

Despite having worked with you for years, Commanders are likely to pass you in the hallway without greeting you, ride the elevator with you without speaking, or encounter you in public without acknowledging you. Their aloofness isn't intended as an offense, but because they aren't at all introspective, they don't realize they're perceived to be rude. It's just that they're otherwise mentally engaged, and the softer side of human interaction isn't a priority for them. Indeed, the feelings of others are nowhere near the top of the priority list for these folks, so ignoring you is their natural, default position.

Commanders are perfectionists who neither expect nor provide praise. In their view, that you do an outstanding job is a reasonable expectation, and your paycheck is adequate praise. If you want more than that, "Go see your mother!" While it's true that they aren't warm and fuzzy, Commanders have a code of honor, manifesting a strong loyalty to their "troops." They'll get down in the trenches alongside their subordinates and get their hands dirty; they don't ask anything that they would not be willing to do themselves; and they protect their people from the criticism of others. Whatever the source of or the cause for criticism, Commanders insert themselves between the complainant and their subordinate, taking the hit themselves. No one but the Commander is allowed to criticize the Commander's subordinates. Don't misunderstand; once behind closed doors, the Commander may indeed read the riot act to a subordinate; but this will be a private interaction to be engaged in only by the Commander boss.

*Julia, a Commander and the new director of a highly successful publications group, has been vocal about her conclusion that staff waste a lot of time. To remedy this, she has been closely scrutinizing staff, monitoring their conversations, peering at their computer screens, and interrupting their collaborations, and she has required everyone to produce a morning to-do list and an afternoon "done" list.*

At all times, Commanders like Julia are on a mission and woe to you if you're in their way or aren't complying with their timetables. They have a sense of immediacy about everything, making every assignment seem as if it's needed yesterday. In their wake is a flurry of activity—papers fluttering and people scrambling furiously to do the Commander's bidding instantly.

Commanders function at a level of intensity that makes most people uncomfortable. Their movements are brisk and purposeful, and they exude a sense of innate power. While it's true that others don't feel warmly toward this style of behavior and probably wouldn't proactively seek social time with them, there is nonetheless a sense of trust that Commanders will behave honorably and manage as fairly as possible. Commanders are not cruel; they're not hostile or bullying, but their strong sense of self-confidence makes them directive, demanding, and distant.

If you should happen to make the mistake of interrupting Commanders, claiming they're wrong, second guessing them, or criticizing them, be prepared for a protracted period of dead silence, augmented by the Commander's unblinking, soul-searing stare, which can ultimately elicit either discomfiture or an appropriate retraction. This same reaction is likely to occur if you engage in behavior, such as fidgeting or squirming, that telegraphs the degree of discipline you're having to impose to prevent yourself from interrupting.

Commanders have a tough time with casual day. Although they're not socially awkward, their presence is heavy and their countenance perpetually serious. They just can't seem to "do" leisure, and are often workaholics, to whom fun seems a foreign concept.

Innovation is really tough for Commanders. Since new ideas can put them at the beginning of a learning curve where mistakes and the absence of mastery are visible to others, Commanders don't easily put themselves in such situations. It's particularly important, when presenting new ideas to Commanders, that you link the innovations to increased order, expanded control, or enhanced results.

*Marie, a Commander administrative assistant, controls the president's calendar. She's a highly organized master scheduler who can choreograph complex travel arrangements, ensuring that even the slightest inconvenience disappears immediately. Under the guise of loyalty to the president, she functions as an impenetrable gatekeeper. She grants access to the president only if she's convinced it would be appropriate and withholds contact information when the president is traveling so that she can control access to him.*

Marie's micromanagement typifies Commanders at their worst. Convinced that allowing others to use their own judgment inevitably produces a suboptimal product, Commanders are explicit about what they want done, how they want it done, when to do it, where to do it, how long to do it, and with whom to do it.

Conservative in dress, investment portfolio, and surroundings, the Commander's domain is always shipshape and without froufrou. Even plants and pictures don't find their way into Commanders' spaces except through the softening influences of a spouse or secretary.

## Greatest Strengths

Commanders are implementers. Results oriented in the extreme, they possess both strategic vision and tactical ability, equipping them to achieve targeted outcomes no matter what. If you want something implemented, just tell the Commander it can't be done, and then step back and prepare to eat their dust. The fact that others think something can't be done, in and of itself, is tremendously motivating to Commanders. Overcoming obstacles is an instinctive ability for Commanders, and their consistent success in doing so elicits confidence from both their superiors and their subordinates. Unflappable in the face of risk, danger, or hostility, Commanders are inspirational, evoking in others a willingness, even a desire, to be led. Aware they might not like the trip and that there may be bloodshed along the way, others are willing to follow the Commander because they believe wherever he or she is headed is, ultimately, the right place to go and that wherever "there" is, the Commander will absolutely get them there.

## Greatest Need

*At an all-staff retreat, employees were grouped into small, multi-hierarchical teams. Within seconds of receiving the team assignment and prior to any discussion with his teammates, Marshal, a manager, jumped up and outlined his solution on the flip chart provided. He then proceeded to explain to the team why regardless of what they might be thinking, his was the optimal and the only worthy solution. Two years later, Marshal is being passed over for promotion to the assistant director position.*

For Marshal, as with most Commanders, control is a necessary means to achieving desired results, with "results" defined by what the Commander believes to be optimal, and with "optimal" defined as something only the Commanders can achieve. Discomfort becomes irritability when their span or degree of control is, in their opinion, encroached upon by others. Convinced that only they themselves can ensure success in an orderly fashion, Commanders interrogate others who are in control of coveted functions to the point of evidencing a complete lack of confidence in their ability. Alleging risk to their own work products when they aren't in control, Commanders adopt a "lock down," bunker-like mentality that either thwarts those in control from moving forward or makes it so painfully arduous that work is often reconfigured to relieve everyone's misery. Control, order, and results are the moment-by-moment focus of Commanders.

## Decision Method

Commanders are supremely self-confident, trusting their own opinions over those of others. Not surprisingly, then, their decisions are based on their own assessments. They expect everyone to do precisely what they say, exactly the way they want it done, immediately. Anything less and the Commander takes action to prevail. The clear message is that anything other than their way is suboptimal.

## Reaction to Feedback

When the Commander chooses retaliation as a response to critical feedback, it's because the feedback was given without the proper packaging technique and/or they perceive an erosion or a loss of their span of control.

There is a right way to give criticism to a Commander—and "directly" definitely isn't it. Remember, the Commander cares most about results, order, and control, so feedback should be expressed within the context of one or more of these values. Here are some examples.

If you are Commander Marie's boss and need her to allow greater access to you, describe how your suggestions will further enhance order, control, and/or results. If you want Commander Marshal to share leadership with another individual, establish explicit outcome measures that cannot be achieved unless leadership is shared.

For the Commander who wants to be evaluated based solely on results without consideration for method, clarify that both outcome and method will be weighed equally at assessment time. Here's a more direct approach that's still adequately packaged: "I'm delighted that you have competence X; I value the competence because it achieves A, B, and C results for us. However, when you overdo that strength the impact is…, and the impact we're shooting for is actually…." Instead of criticizing the Commander's behavior, clarify the difference between the results he or she achieved and the results desired. Commanders will listen to feedback if it's grounded in improving results, increasing order, and/or expanding control.

**Now go to the Predictive Grid on page 15 and enter a score from 5 to 25 in column B, indicating the degree to which you fit the Commander description.**

## Managing Vulnerabilities to the Commander Superior

As your boss, Commanders make you vulnerable by not delegating substantive assignments, thereby dwarfing the scope, depth, and speed of your growth. They loathe delegation because

- You can't possibly do it as well as they can.
- It'll take longer to explain to you how to do it than to do it themselves.
- The probability of your making an error is too great.
- They can't afford for their results or timelines to be impeded by the possibility of your error.

To get challenging assignments, you'll need to work to earn the Commander's trust. Do this by looking for every opportunity to demonstrate initiative in ways that show you're thinking as the Commander would (which, of course, is the right way to think—and, indeed, the only way to think). Constantly ask yourself, "What comes next?" and do it without waiting to be asked. Here are a few examples.

There's a meeting coming up for which you can reasonably anticipate that your Commander boss might want any one of three presentations, files, or outlines. Have all three prepared and ready to go in advance. If a letter has to go out from your Commander boss to convey one of three different messages, prepare all three for signature in advance. If a contract is to be awarded to an external expert who has to meet certain criteria, without waiting to being asked, prepare overviews of at least three candidates, all of whom are qualified, including assessments of additional criteria you believe your Commander boss may value. Weight these additional criteria consistent with how you believe your boss would prioritize them.

It's true that going to all this trouble takes additional time, but it earns you the Commander's trust and, therefore, the delegation of challenging assignments for three important reasons: First, it demonstrates initiative, a characteristic Commanders highly value in their subordinates. Second, it demonstrates that you're willing to do the extra work, willing to earn better assignments. Third, it indicates that your values and your thinking are in alignment with the Commander's own.

## Adapting Techniques for Interacting With the Commander Boss

- **Clean up your act.** Orderliness is the most basic precursor to trustworthiness for Commanders, and they make judgments about your abilities based on both the appearance of your workspace and your personal appearance.

It is not sufficient that you can put your hand on something in mere seconds; if it looks like a bomb hit your office, the Commander will judge you as sloppy and will not delegate to you. Ladies, if you wear short skirts, have runs in your stockings, show cleavage, wear stiletto heels, sport bejeweled nails, or chew gum, the Commander's trust will never be yours. Gentlemen, if there's more than one crease in each pants leg or shirt sleeve, if skin shows above your socks when you cross you legs, if your shoes aren't

shined, if your shirt doesn't quite make it all the way around your tummy without making your buttons gape, if your collars and hems are frayed, the Commander's trust will never be yours either. Remember: If the Commander judges you as sloppy, he or she won't delegate to you. So sit up straight. No slouching! No boisterous behavior! Developing successful working relationships with Commanders requires impeccable, conservative appearance and elocution coupled with behavior that avoids both real and perceived impropriety.

- **Give the bad news up front.** If you have bad news to deliver, just bottom line your Commander boss. Two pet peeves of Commanders are excuses and long explanations about why something went awry. They don't care why it happened and they don't care whose fault it was. They just want to know what you are going to do to fix it and what you're going to do to prevent a recurrence. So don't shift the blame onto someone else or try to otherwise sidestep responsibility. Be direct and brief, and for goodness sake, don't cry. Avoid phrases such as "I think," or "we'll see," or "we're trying to," or "we hope." Limit your briefing to what you know and what you're going to do. Don't let their rapid-fire questions push you into making commitments you can't honor or providing answers you'll later have to retract. Ideally, you'll have a solution already in progress, so you can tell the Commander what you already have done about a situation. If this isn't possible, at least be prepared with a recommended solution. Do not try to rationalize, excuse, or trivialize errors. Doing so will just infuriate the Commander. Instead, step up to the plate and take the blame even if it isn't your fault, then focus on next steps with timelines.

- **Don't emotionalize anything.** Don't show emotion in your facial expressions, body language, or tone of voice. Eliminate emotion-laden words.

For example, instead of referring to poor morale, talk about the anticipated results and impacts of improved morale. You may have to reformat how you express yourself to meet this standard, and this takes a bit of extra effort, but you'll be more effective by doing so.

- **Assess.** When you have to present something to your Commander boss for a decision, create a chart with the choices shown as rows and the advantages and disadvantages as columns. This is effective because it allows the Commander to make the decision. Be sure to let the Commander know which of the choices you recommend, but prepare the matrix so that it's easy for the Commander to see that you've properly analyzed the choices.

- **Get in and out quickly.** Don't just waltz into the Commander's office and sit down. Sitting implies either that you plan to stay a while, when they just want to dispense with you, or that you want to chat, and Commanders don't "do" chat. In both written and verbal communication, provide the executive summary first; be brief, clear, and succinct. Prepare so well for your interactions with your Commander that you're in and out quickly—"in" only when there's substantive reason and "out" quickly through thorough preparation. If the Commander wants more information, rest assured it will be asked of you.

- **Just do it!** Anticipate next steps and take appropriate action. On a moment-by-moment basis, ask yourself what the Commander would do next. Anticipate questions, objections, and consequences, and then take action. DO IT! Don't wait to be asked and don't ask permission to take initiative. Take it! With Commanders, it's better to apologize for having taken a wrong action than to try to explain having done nothing. Even if the Commander ultimately overturns your decision or criticizes your decision, he or she will respect you for having had the courage to act, especially if you continue to do so after having failed.

- **Create options.** In case the Commander rejects your Plan A for whatever it is you want to accomplish, have Plan B already prepared in your hip pocket. Be ready as well with Plan C in case the Commander rejects Plan B. Don't wait to be instructed to make revisions. Anticipate the revisions or the alternatives the Commander may want, and prepare them in advance.

- **Stand up for yourself.** Nothing earns a Commander's lack of respect more quickly than wimping out or running scared. Don't be afraid to stand up to your Commander; don't cower, give up, or walk away at the first "no." Don't permit yourself to be intimidated by the Commander. Without being insubordinate, don't hesitate to put up a fight for what you believe in (assuming, of course, that your idea is well grounded in improved results, increased order, or expanded control). The Commander may never agree with you, but he or she will respect your mettle.

- **Link everything to control, order, and/or results.** Do this, and you're most likely to get whatever it is you want from the Commander. If you fail to establish this linkage, not only will you not get what you want, you won't even get the Commander's attention. Whether you want a raise, more responsibility, a different title or office, if you cannot link what you want to increased order, control, or results, then you're wasting your breath.

## Managing Vulnerability to the Commander Subordinate

As your subordinates, Commanders will be your greatest blessings or your worst nightmares, depending almost entirely on how you manage them. They're likely to exhibit behavior that in their view merely demonstrates initiative and drive but could be interpreted as attempting to take over your job. They look for opportunities to take initiative and will reach out for more and more responsibility, demonstrating their competence and testing the limits of their authority. Although chastising them for not knowing their place may be the natural reaction, doing so will cause a Commander subordinate to go around you, behind you, over you, through you, or out the door, none of which is desirable. If you want these folks in your corner, giving you the best they have to offer on a consistent basis, then delegate substantively to your Commander subordinates. Establish parameters within which you want your subordinates to perform, but having articulated these, delegate!

To effectively manage Commanders, you must first recognize that they usually are competent to handle additional responsibility and would welcome it. Articulate the desired results, and then stand aside and let Commanders figure out the how-to's. Commanders need to demonstrate their capabilities. They want to strut their stuff for you and show you how good they are. Depriving them of such opportunities isn't an effective choice. Relinquishing a project to them helps meet their need for control and motivates them to perform at their best.

## Adapting Techniques for Interacting With the Commander Subordinate

- **Delegate**. Make challenging work assignments that show you trust the judgment of your Commander subordinate.

- **Don't micromanage.** Avoid telling your Commander subordinates how to complete the work. Instead, articulate only the desired outcome and let them figure out how to get it done.

- **Put Commanders in positions of leadership.** Consider allowing them to be team leaders, to staff committees, to present to the board, and to supervise projects or people.

- **Ask for Commanders' opinions.** Describe a complex situation, and invite them to tell you how they would handle it. Implement or critique their suggestion as appropriate. Do this often.

- **Be explicit about Commanders' career paths.** By doing so, you put them in control of their pace and progress.

- **Distinguish controllers from Commanders.** Be alert to the possibility that your subordinate may be just a controlling personality that others find intrusive and noncollaborative. Monitor whether your subordinate is a mature Commander, making sound decisions and taking appropriate initiatives.

- **Ask Commanders to improve something.** Identify a system or process in need of overhaul and let your Commander make revisions. Better yet, ask your Commander to identify the system or process that needs to be improved.

- **Back decisions whenever possible.** Even if a Commander's decision isn't optimal, back it if you can. Certainly you should help a Commander see the other options and share how you would have evaluated those options, but try not to overturn decisions.

## Other Styles Commanders Find Most Challenging

- Drifter's lack of focus and reliability
- Avoider's reticence to take initiative or risk
- Performer's subordination of substance to glitz and puffery

## Actual 360-Degree Input on Commanders

Because Commanders want to be valued and validated for their ability to deliver results, they consistently demonstrate a prioritization of results over people. The 360-degree input below is replete with evidence that others are keenly aware of this.

### Here's what their superiors have to say:

- *Doesn't delegate well, wants to be involved in everything when he should move away from the administrative issues that could be left to others.*

- *Bulldozes over those who disagree without determining if disagreement has validity.*

- *Can be overzealous. Is inexhaustible. Single-minded intensity makes others uncomfortable.*

- *When she has "signed up," she'll do nothing halfway and expects the same from others.*

- *Articulates and demonstrates disesteem for the need to schmooze—which is, to a great extent, how things get done in our business.*

- *Absolute imperviousness to distractions. Ignores everyone and everything unless they can advance the ball. Becomes a loner if colleagues aren't as driven or committed.*

- *The pace of her work is extremely demanding. Her competence actually terrifies those who aren't as focused. Should realize that others are worthy even if they can't rise to her level or work at her pace.*

### Here's what their peers have to say:

- *In an effort to "reveal" to someone what would solve their problem, she interrogates them, thinking she's being helpful, when in fact she's being obnoxious.*

- *Is an absolutist. There's only black and white—no gray. Must prevail. Undertakes campaign-like approach to getting his way.*

- *It requires real effort to befriend this person, even professionally. Seems cold and insensitive.*

- *Overconfident; makes snap judgments that aren't optimal. Warp speed multitasking results in missing important details.*

- *Sense of immediacy makes others ill at ease. Such a strong personality that others are reluctant to actively participate in discussions and debates with him.*

- *Imposes will rather than winning others over. If she can't convince others toward her point of view easily and quickly, she has no qualms whatsoever about sacrificing relationships or becoming contemptuous.*

## Here's what their subordinates have to say:

- *Overextends us and undersupports us. Unapproachable regarding obstacles that may have prevented optimal performance and has zero interest in what it takes to get the job done.*

- *We are made to feel like underachievers for putting in only 40 hours per week.*

- *Is constantly checking up on staff to find out who is where. Believes we're always trying to get away with something. Can't resist meddling. Exudes negativity toward anyone who is having fun, as if they aren't really working.*

- *Creates a sense of futility by undermining authority. She thinks nothing of unilaterally reversing her decisions, abandoning prior agreements at whim, taking personnel actions without consultation—all with total disregard for the consequences of her actions. This creates feelings of bitterness, disillusionment, impotence, and anger.*

- *Passion is micromanaged out of us every single day. I'm not permitted to think on my own, despite my credentials and experience. He makes every decision, no matter how small. This impedes my professional growth and creates a growing sense of apathy about my work. I have zero input, so why should I care about the outcome?*

- *Micromanages but undersupervises. Doesn't supply clear direction or keep us in the loop, so time is wasted in rework. Never has time for us, seems to consider it a burden to have to keep others informed.*

# CHAPTER 3

# The Drifter

**DESCRIPTORS**

FREE-SPIRITED

CREATIVE, IMPROVISES

EASY GOING, LAID BACK

NOT AN IMPLEMENTER

HATES RULES, FACTS

NO FOLLOW-UP OR COMPLETION

CHANGES SUBJECT FREQUENTLY

NO STRONG VALUES

DISORGANIZED, CHAOTIC

IMPULSIVE

AMBIGUOUS, CONFUSING

IMAGINATIVE

OPEN TO ALL STIMULI

NOT FOCUSED

NEEDS SENSATION, NEWNESS

FRIENDLY, WARM

*O*BLIVIOUS TO THE RADIAL IMPACTS OF *doing so, Christopher, a senior vice president, vacates policy and changes personnel decisions made by direct reports based on… Actually, no one seems to be able to discern the basis for such decisions. All that's clear is that any decision made by any one of his direct reports can be overturned at any moment, and he may or may not remember to tell that direct report about it. Requests for leave are granted after having been denied by supervisors, new titles are created and job functions are changed on the spur of the moment, and almost daily he thinks of new initiatives that divert time and attention from existing projects.*

Virtually antithetical to Commanders, Drifters such as Christopher seem unable to comply with even the most fundamental components of structure in the workplace. Disorganized, impulsive, even chaotic, Drifters cannot be relied on to honor business commitments, whether to a deadline, a project, a job, or an employer. Their appearance is almost always somewhat mussed and disheveled, as is their workspace. Predictably tardy and chronically absent, their physical presence often belies their cognitive attention, since they are perpetually on a mental frolic that has nothing to do with the reason their participation was requested.

Somehow, wherever the Drifter has been for any length of time becomes a disaster area. It's not that they intend to leave chaos in their wake, but they do. In fact, it is the perpetual absence of specific intent that blinds Drifters to the chaos they create. They change the subject often, either because they're giving voice to their thoughts in real time or because they've already forgotten what you were talking about.

What seems to others like deliberate noncompliance or a disregard for policy and procedures manuals is actually obliviousness. Drifters simply have no awareness of the need for structure, and are truly amazed at the degree to which others allow structure to constrain and confine their lives. Indeed, Drifters feel a pained sympathy for the uptight, "straight-jacketed" majority, for whom their most ardent wish would be the ability to "chill." In their view, the best use of policy and procedures manuals is as door stops.

All your efforts to carefully write executive summaries or clearly articulate instructions will be lost on Drifters. In handing documents to them, you may as well have tossed them into the wind, since they lose or misplace everything they touch. They barely scan documents, retaining nothing, so you're endlessly repeating yourself. When collaborating on projects, Drifters' extremely short attention span and mental "flitting about" results in missed details and deadlines, failure to follow up, and incomplete work.

*Corrine, a director, routinely makes commitments when communicating with member and nonmember external constituencies. Because she has no understanding of or appreciation for existing work or resource availability, she is dumbfounded when staff complain about the requisite work or rework generated by her commitments, To her, these commitments are "no big deal," merely requiring someone to "just do this" or "just do that." Exasperated, frustrated, and frenetic, her team is perpetually scrambling to preserve her credibility by delivering what she promises.*

Corrine's intent isn't to create havoc but to be accommodating. To her, as with other Drifters, change is to be welcomed. They respond well to change, and even instigate it, if only to disrupt routine. It's easy to understand why Corrine's Drifter behavior would be exasperating for her colleagues. Indeed, of all the behavior types, Drifters are the most difficult for most others. Their insatiable desire for constant entertainment, their lack of structured thought, and their unrealistic need for perpetual fun can be an ongoing source of aggravation.

Depicting the essence of Drifter behavior is the senior vice president who, having been told by her CEO not to pick up the alcohol tab at a particular member event, asked a peer to do so. The CEO confronted the peer, who explained that the Drifter had made the request, and hadn't mentioned the CEO's instruction. The Drifter's response to the CEO's subsequent confrontation was that she had indeed complied with his instruction, in that she had not been the one who paid for the alcohol.

Much like the character Dennis the Menace, Drifters have warm and friendly dispositions; they're happy-go-lucky, laid back, free-spirited, and easy going. They live life in the moment, by impulse, with no instructive memories to constrain them and no future view to direct them. Endlessly distracted, Drifters take spontaneous detours from current tasks and responsibilities to explore what's happening elsewhere. Their receptivity to and need for constant and varied stimulation makes them susceptible to sensory overload, a state they relish at the expense of attentiveness.

This lack of focus and resulting noncompliance to the most basic business norms can include even the conversation they had five minutes ago. When confronted by aggravated others, Drifters are truly mystified that anyone would be irritated by such small things. Needless to say, Drifters don't typically have military backgrounds—at least not by choice.

*Jackson, the CEO, has an aversion to planning and makes what he considers to be good-natured fun of the annual goal-setting process. Despite repeated requests from the senior team to develop a three-year strategic plan, he just won't entertain substantive discussion beyond the next 90 days. If present when others engage in discussion that devolves into long-range planning, he becomes disruptive, petulant, and capricious.*

Jackson's problematic behavior demonstrates that because Drifters think conceptually, they usually aren't good planners. They don't give a moment of thought to the potential consequences of their behavior and fail to develop next steps toward targeted achievements. They miss deadlines, overlook details, and fail to follow up. They seem to hear only what they want to hear, conveniently editing the rest to align with their preferences.

When formal meetings hold Drifters captive, most of what is said goes in one ear and out the other. Their eyes glaze over, and they can't keep listening because they're playing a much more engaging game or movie in their heads. Meetings have to be highly entertaining and must appeal to multiple senses to have any hope of attracting or retaining Drifters' attention.

Because they have no strong doctrine to which they adamantly adhere, Drifters are refreshingly nonjudgmental of others. However, their unprincipled lack of strong tenets also makes them unpredictable, confusing, ambiguous, even fickle, often viewed to be wholly unsuitable for any business environment.

*At least one prediction was reliably true of any meeting conducted by Stacey: He would invariably wander onto numerous irrelevant subjects, never stimulated by obvious segues, further confirming his already well known reputation for wasting huge amounts of others' time. Despite great difficulty in finding mutually available times to meet and with complete disregard for tight agendas packed with high-profile projects needing major decisions, his long-winded monologues about his pet projects hijacked productivity, earned him the disrespect and resentment of an exasperated staff, and made others question both his intellect and his utility.*

You may well interpret Stacey's lack of focus and structure as adolescent characteristics, concluding that Drifters aren't often found in positions of authority. Think again. Their affability, unpretentiousness, low stress level even in times of crisis, and relaxed demeanor even amid the extreme formality of others are often seen to be just what the doctor ordered—particularly when high-performance executives who don't need a lot of supervision are the Drifter's direct reports.

## Greatest Strengths

Drifters are the most creative and imaginative of all behavior styles. They're playwrights, speechwriters, authors, musicians, inventors, innovators, designers, comedians, dancers, facilitators of experiential retreats for whom alignment between vocation and avocation is essential.

Drifters can envision a cohesive whole from mere fragments, effortlessly improvise bridges where others see only chasms, see all different points of view, and devise brilliantly simple solutions to seemingly insurmountable problems. To the extent the success of your organization depends on innovation, the Drifter's capabilities can be a crucial resource. They come up with ideas that no one else would ever conceive, precisely because they don't recognize the constraints that are obvious to others.

Casually, almost incidentally, Drifters conceive stunning, blockbuster ideas, and with a generosity that seems borne of naiveté, they plop these ideas out there for others to implement. An off-the-wall suggestion from a Drifter can revitalize mature products, breathe life into a stale membership campaign, rejuvenate and energize key stakeholders, or bring into existence a new product or service that expands organizational reach and increases nondues revenue. Although the myriad, positive business implications of Drifters' ideas may be immediately clear to others, Drifters don't seem impressed. When, intending to compliment Drifters, you start listing the benefits or solutions enabled by their suggestions, the response may be a seemingly unaffected, "That's cool," and off they drift in search of another sensory-rich, multifaceted opportunity. That there are beneficiaries of their ideas isn't sufficiently interesting to sustain Drifters' attention; their joy lies in creation, not in recognition or implementation.

## Greatest Need

What Drifters need most is freedom. Almost physiologically, they cannot abide structure, confinement, rules, regulations, policies, procedures, deadlines, or even ordinary conventions. Further, commitment is antithetical to their wiring. Drifters may leave their jobs on impulse, if for no reason other than a desire for new surroundings. If you manage a Drifter, this need for freedom has numerous implications for the types of assignments you make, the duration and location of these assignments, and the activities in which you include the Drifter. If you report to a Drifter, this need has implications for clarity of assignments, structure of your job, and the internal reputation of your department.

## Decision Method

No decision is considered final by Drifters. Irreverent about the formality of decision making, their attitude is, "Who cares? In a few years, it won't make a difference anyway, so flip a coin! And don't worry; be happy!" Drifters don't spend time developing criteria for decision making; they consider it unnecessary, since situations and petitioners could change.

Whatever decisions Drifters have made in the past are unreliable predictors of future decisions. Whether this is because they can't recall what was previously agreed to or because they just had a new idea that requires abandoning the earlier decision, their flexibility in decision making can be counterproductive, causing redundancy and rework.

## Reaction to Feedback

Upon receiving critical feedback, the Drifter's apologetic countenance implies an innocence that can be completely disarming, since, obviously, their oversight bore you no ill intent. They don't pay attention long enough to form intent.

Imposing a negative consequence of any kind is ineffective with Drifters. They float through setbacks—in fact, they float through life—in a near dreamlike state, vaguely baffled by the tenseness of others. To the Drifters' way of thinking, life should be a veritable picnic, so when unpleasantness occurs, they simply take an imaginary sojourn until the complainants recover.

If you become angry, the Drifter will graciously assume you just need some space, slip away to give you time to recuperate, and won't hold your angry outburst against you. To Drifters, nothing they did or didn't do was really at issue; you were just having a bad day and they believe everything will be OK in a day or two.

If you impose penalties on Drifters, realize that doing so won't change their behavior. They'll find a way to offset any punishment you devise. The only effective way to gain compliance from Drifters is to use personal appeals. If you make Drifters aware that their behavior is about to cause negative consequences for you or others, Drifters are likely to comply. They may be impervious to the reprimands they've brought upon themselves, but their caring natures prevent them from knowingly getting others in trouble.

**Now go to the Predictive Grid on page 15 and enter a score from 5 to 25 in column B, indicating the degree to which you fit the Drifter description.**

## Managing Vulnerability to the Drifter Superior

As your boss, the Drifter makes you vulnerable by not providing any structure. Even if your Drifter boss has received instructions from above, it's entirely possible he or she won't remember to implement. So, heads up! This means they'll make commitments to you and forget to honor them. Drifters will agree, for example, to instruct others, to reign in others, to discipline others, and then become involved in something else they find more engaging. Thus diverted, Drifter bosses will forget to act and will be genuinely oblivious when you remind them of their commitments.

To cope successfully with a Drifter boss, you'll need to provide your own structure. The bad news is that you'll have to write, for example, your own job description and your own performance review. The good news is that Drifters will gratefully sign and approve pretty much anything you write, and you'll have plenty of freedom to take initiative.

Even as bosses, Drifters are notoriously disorganized, and others may impute to you these same traits simply because you work for a Drifter. Use your organizing abilities to protect your Drifter boss, and to make him or her look good.

Better to recognize that there is opportunity in shoring up his or her weaknesses than to resist and resent his or her haphazardness.

Don't expect a lot of feedback from Drifter bosses. They don't pay attention to anything long enough to really assess it. And don't be insulted or aggravated by their inattentiveness. The fact that your Drifter boss isn't focused on you and your career doesn't mean you can't take control of your own professional trajectory, your own targeted outcomes, and seek input elsewhere.

## Adapting Techniques for Interaction With Drifter Superiors

- **Don't let hierarchy impede** the establishment of a sense of collaborative comradeship around the work. Drifter bosses aren't distracted by titles and enjoy working with anyone who isn't uptight.

- **Don't assume Drifters are aware** of the etiquette and unspoken peeves or mores of the board or other groups. Prepare them. And in so doing, be explicit. Empathize, but be explicit!

- **Don't submit lengthy documents** to your Drifter boss. Although you may need to keep such documents for your own files, verbal overviews work best for the Drifter.

- **Do all you can to reduce the need for direction** from your Drifter boss and to take as much off the Drifter boss's plate as you can.

- **Avoid engaging your Drifter boss in long-range planning** sessions. Do the planning, of course, but don't expect your boss to show up, to formally integrate short-term initiatives with the plan, or to be interested in reading the plan. Planning is tedious for Drifters, and since they prefer to stay flexible, they see it as less worthwhile than most others do. You can be aggravated by the conclusion that this constitutes abdication of responsibility on your boss's part, or you can set aside your aggravation, which isn't effective anyway, and just get about the business of shoring up his or her weakness in this area.

- **Think before asking your Drifter boss for a decision.** Format clear recommendations from which the Drifter boss can easily choose. This will help reduce the likelihood of tangential conversations.

- **Strive to conduct conversations with your Drifter boss** in different venues. Mix it up. Schedule meetings in different offices or different restaurants or take your Drifter boss on a walk around the building to talk about a business problem or opportunity.

- **Make suggestions that the Drifter boss would enjoy** implementing, such as a casual day or contests with rewards delivered by the Drifter boss.

- **Offer to take on the facets of the Drifter's job** that you know she or he would find tedious.

## Managing Vulnerability to the Drifter Subordinate

Such unconventional methods are required to successfully manage the Drifter subordinate that others may question your tactics. The only response that's at least partially defensible is that you're managing everyone as individuals, without eroding business results.

Drifter subordinates make you vulnerable by not completing assignments on time, often not even remembering that you gave them assignments. Other employees, especially those who are more structured, resent the Drifter's behavior. Make sure your staff understand that, for each of them, you are committed to aligning their strengths with their tasks. Make sure they understand one another's abilities and how those strengths contribute to overall success.

Making work fun for the Drifter really is essential, and doing so on a consistent basis may seem impractical, unrealistic, or too difficult. But take heart. Remember that both Einstein and Edison were once expelled from elementary school for their Drifter behaviors!

So, how do you optimize interacting with this behavior style in the real workplace? After all, most business environments are highly structured, requiring specific outcomes by specific dates. What hope is there for working successfully with someone whose head is always in the clouds? As unrealistic and impossible as it may seem, following are tips for doing just that.

Many of you are likely to have a hard time with the suggestions you're about to read. You might think, "This isn't kindergarten; this is work. Drifters have to adapt!" Keep that attitude and not only will you fail to get discretionary energy from the Drifter, you'll also fail to get the best the Drifter has to offer. The effectiveness of these techniques is not contingent upon your esteem for them. They work—whether you like them or not. Subordinate your emotional reaction to these tips, and use them because they work.

## Adapting Techniques for Interacting With Drifter Subordinates

- **Keep the work context light-hearted** and upbeat, not heavy and punitive. Create a sense of enjoyment for the work as opposed to establishing a must do/ should do environment.

- **Be OK with your Drifter's incorporating his or her personality** and pizzazz into the work environment. Allow for the Drifter's own brand of idiosyncrasy. Depending on what their job functions are, it could be perfectly fine that they have more body parts pierced than you have hairs on your head; it could be of no consequence that they have visible tattoos or that their hair color is extreme. Drifters don't conform to norms, and if you elevate conformance over skills and abilities, it's tantamount to crushing their spirits. As a result, you won't retain the gifts Drifters have to offer, because you won't retain the Drifters. Articulate but minimize any necessary constraints.

- **Be physiologically at rest.** If your brow is furrowed and your lips are pursed and your physiology is aggressive, judgmental, stiff, and stressed, the Drifter is just going to tune you out. Spontaneous mental detachment is a reflex for Drifters. They may be in a one-on-one meeting with you, looking right at you without hearing a word you say.

- **Structure work assignments** so that they can be completed in segments. Drifters are at their best with short, compact periods of concentration, so break projects down into component parts and assign them separately. For example, first ask a graphic designer to do a logo, then a cover, then the text layout for a project, rather than handing over the entire project at once.

- **Use "what if" scenarios.** Drifter subordinates have trouble seeing beyond right now. Instead of demanding that they learn to anticipate, engage them in "what if" conversations. Instead of expecting them to forecast, ask them to "dream" with you for a bit.

- **Provide lots of variety in the work** Drifters do, where they do it, even with whom they work. For example, let them work in the conference room one day, in the office of a vacationing employee the next, in the library the next day, with a team the next. Rather than keeping them tasked on Project A through to its conclusion, segment their work among multiple projects.

- **Tap their imagination.** Ask for advice from the Drifter when you initially engage in some new endeavor, when you have a particularly vexing problem, or when you're looking for ideas for new products or services.

- **Do the unexpected.** Hold a meeting outside; host a pot-luck lunch; consider humorous contests; have interactive brown-bag sessions.

- **Ask the Drifter subordinate to create** ways to display progress toward targeted outcomes. For example, a large whiteboard could be used to post relevant milestones. Someone else may be better at establishing and tracking the milestones, but the Drifter can create and maintain a great-looking scoreboard (color coded, of course!) and his or her enthusiasm will rally others around its purpose.

- **Develop a sense of humor.** Write notes in crayon; tape cartoons to the Drifter's computer; leave funny messages on voicemail. Make fun of yourself. Be silly occasionally. Display the ability to just kick back and relate.

- **Remember that sensory overload is bliss** to Drifters. Don't be surprised if the Drifter works with a muted TV visible or wears iPod headphones to listen to music while working.

- **Value and validate Drifters for their innovation** and creativity, their ability to improvise on a moment's notice, and their out-of-the-box thinking.

- **Consider allowing your Drifter to handle** what others find distracting. Perhaps there are interruptions or frequent but not time-consuming activities that could be shed to the Drifter. Rather than feeling put upon, the Drifter craves work that adds to the variety in the workday.

## Other Styles Drifters Find Most Challenging
- Commanders' omnipresent need for structure
- Attackers' rage
- Analyticals' insatiable need for data, evidence, proof

## Actual 360-Degree Input on Drifters
Drifters just can't resist daydreaming. They want to be valued and validated for their creativity and innovation. To their way of thinking, failing to deliver measurable, on-time results is an acceptable price to pay for keeping their imagination fresh. This 360-degree input on Drifters reveals the frustration others have with this style.

## Here's what their superiors have to say:

- *Needs to focus. Gets distracted by interesting things that are not related to her work. Just not possible to wade through the morass of mental pinball to get needed information.*

- *Written and verbal communications are not structured or crisp. Disjointed, riddled with filler words and phrases that have no meaning.*

- *There is no consistency in performance or in the application of policies.*

- *Relies too heavily on other people. Often caught off guard; fails to anticipate and prepare.*

- *Has lots of great ideas; however, does not implement them.*

- *Her deliverables are rarely in the format requested; indeed there is rarely a format or structure to her deliverables.*

## Here's what their peers have to say:

- *Doesn't pay any attention to tracking or understanding trends or other metrics; therefore, doesn't understand our challenges and can't offer useful assistance. Does not evaluate, assess, analyze, solve. Just floats through.*

- *Ambiguous about everything. Personifies "vague." Can't nail this person down on anything. Forgets what he promises, fails to keep others informed, is always late, has to be hounded to meet deadlines.*

- *Head in the clouds. Must be told something multiple times before it sinks in. Spacey. Wishy-washy.*

- *Her presentations are totally unstructured; they just go on and on without much substance. This isn't casual extemporaneousness—it's irresponsible sloppiness.*

- *He's so disorganized—and it's visible to our committees. They don't get materials till the day before, and even then agendas aren't honored. Constantly gets sidetracked. Has utter disdain for preparedness, agenda, or structure of any kind.*

- *Can't seem to say anything concrete. Equivocates. Blurs. I leave this person knowing less than when the conversation began.*

### Here's what their subordinates have to say:

- *My boss erodes my productivity every day. We waste a lot of time covering old ground: rebriefing, re-explaining, redeciding. Meetings are even suspended while we produce emergency reprints of whatever he has lost. Provides conflicting instructions to different people; it's chaos.*

- *Failure to stay current with emails, voicemails, memos. Ultimately creates crushing avalanches of work.*

- *Thinks out loud, often contradicting what he said earlier. Creates confusion, erodes focus.*

- *Never any finality to his decisions. His views continually evolve, creating endless iterations of previous decisions. Spontaneous changes are rationalized, even when they obliterate weeks of work. Written materials have to be reviewed by others to avoid mixed messages.*

- *During meetings, she digs through her purse unable to find what she's looking for; rummages through papers unable to find what she's looking for. Is perpetually distracted.*

- *Doesn't provide us with guidance, clear instructions, or any type of criteria for success. We're just expected to get into the flow. Definitely not an inspiring leader.*

# CHAPTER 4

# The Attacker

DESCRIPTORS

HOSTILE, ANGRY
INTIMIDATING
REBELLIOUS
ARGUMENTATIVE
DEMORALIZING
STACCATO RATE OF SPEECH
PERSONALLY BELITTLING
CAUSTIC, SEARING, SARCASTIC

GROUCHY
CYNICAL
DEFIANT
SUPERIORITY COMPLEX
SEEKS FAULT IN OTHERS
BLAME ORIENTED
DEAF TO YOUR SIDE OF THE STORY

*H*AVING FIRMLY ESTABLISHED HERSELF (AT LEAST *in her own mind) as the appropriate judge and jury of everyone else in the organization, Director Eleanor routinely demeaned and diminished others in the organization. No interaction with her was completed without her having said, "you should have known…"; "how could you have thought…"; "it would have been obvious to anyone that…"; "even you should have realized that…." When provided with data that captured the impact of her behavior on others, she was surprised but undaunted. She had thought her behavior demonstrated high intellect and was unaware that she was considered abusive. Despite the diagnosis, she was self-validating and in reviewing specific instances of her behavior, reiterated her perception of the appropriateness of her remarks. The chaffing of others, despite the unanimity of negative perceptions about her behavior, was, to Eleanor's way of thinking, completely irrelevant.*

As Eleanor's behavior makes painfully clear, Attackers view themselves as superior to others, continually expressing contempt and disgust for the incompetence and inadequacy of their fellow workers. They are keenly aware of others' shortcomings and keep track of and showcase the mistakes of errant others with the intention of embarrassing them in public. It's not enough for only Attackers to know how stupid and worthless you are; they want everyone to know it. They haven't fulfilled their fiduciary responsibility to protect the world from you until your humiliation is made public at about 80,000 decibels. Using demeaning and condescending tones wrapped in biting sarcasm, they have an arsenal of insults always ready. Everything about Attackers—their voices, eye contact, and body posture—is intimidating and is deliberately used to demoralize everyone with whom they come in contact. Caustic and belittling, cynical and abrasive, their permanent scowls and perpetual, palpable hostility combine to make them the most destructive influence in the workplace. The Greek origin of the word *sarcastic* is *sarkazo*, which means "tearing little strips of flesh." Attackers delight in the verbal equivalent.

Pregnant with your first child? Don't expect congratulations from the Attacker. More likely, the Attacker will point out your thoughtlessness in failing to plan around the important event that's already on the calendar and with which your due date conflicts. Need time off to attend a funeral? Don't expect sympathy from the Attacker. In fact, expect to be made to feel guilty. After all, "There's nothing you can do about a dead person, but there's plenty to do around here!" Deliberately intimidating, Attackers want you shaking on the way into the office and crying on the way out. As they see it, the more terrified you are, the greater the evidence in support of their managerial effectiveness. Erupting at people and things without apparent justification, Attackers are the personification of "going ballistic." Their default position is accusatory. If they can't find something, it doesn't occur to them that they may have misplaced it; instead, their first assumption is that someone must have stolen it; if they can't get something they need, others are conspiring to withhold it; if someone makes a mistake, he or she did so intentionally to embarrass the Attacker. In confronting the accused, the Attacker's staccato rate of speech and bullet-like delivery evince a prosecutorial zeal that is hateful in both language and behavior.

*For John, a vice president, the mistakes of others are personal insults. Red, felt-tipped pen edits would frequently include the word "stupid!" He made a point of letting his own staff know in great detail about the mistakes of others, creating department-wide disesteem for colleagues in other groups. Even when complaints about him rose to the CEO's attention and John was called on the carpet for his behavior, with imperiousness he maintained that his behavior was justified.*

No matter how tough or thick-skinned you are, scathing, vicious attacks like John's can be delivered with an intensity that instantaneously takes your breath away. And in the Attacker's world, there simply isn't any such thing as your side of the story. Your perspective is viewed by Attackers as being completely irrelevant and without value, so, they deduce, giving you an opportunity to present your case would be a colossal waste of time.

Attackers are extremely agitated by peace and tranquility and deride this state of being in others. They can sense serenity creeping into the workplace and swing into action immediately to beat it back. They'll deploy their argumentative and defiant natures deliberately, as a technique for re-establishing the state of severe discord they find more comfortable. That these behaviors make others avoid them isn't something they have to withstand. In fact, being ostracized is as comfortable to Attackers as a pair of old slippers. From multiple significant others in their young lives, they heard negative messages such as you're a pest; go away and leave me alone; you'll never amount to anything; you should be more like so-and-so. They grew up expecting more of the same, preparing for more of the same, and becoming predisposed to exhibit more of the same, and they lost their sensitivity to others in the process.

Attackers see themselves as accomplished warriors, see life as requiring warriors, and consider the exhibition of warrior behavior to be a peak life experience. Bored by the absence of conflict, fearful they'll be seen as "going soft" if they aren't perpetually flexing their warrior muscles, they'll create conflict if necessary to "stay in shape."

*Leah, a senior director, uses every disagreement with her peers as an opportunity to publicly decry their decisions. Whenever she doesn't get her way, she derides and criticizes them to other individuals in group meetings attended by both peers and subordinates. No venue is, in her view, an inappropriate place to vent her disdain for others. Perhaps even more destructive is that with every criticism, she imputes deliberateness and ill intent in an apparent effort to establish her superior wisdom and to diminish others.*

Attackers have a near physiological need to know who is to blame when something goes awry. As Leah's behavior demonstrates, if a mistake has been made at the office, Attackers become mission-driven to track down and expose whoever is at fault. There's no such thing as a cold case file in an environment where the Attacker reigns. Hunting down and convicting the guilty party becomes their raison d'etre, and they'll never give up.

If Attackers are in a traffic jam, they'll straddle the creeper lane, straining to see what idiot caused it. Attackers experience an overwhelming, irrepressible fixation on establishing a clear line of sight to the offending party, and the culprit had better be in need of an ambulance! Once they see the enemy, the one who had the audacity to be in an accident or the stupidity to have car trouble, they can direct their venomous outpouring of verbal abuse with laser-like intensity. This has the effect of confirming (if only in their own minds) their superiority over the great, blubbering masses of humanity and vindicates their denigrating sneer as they drive past, seething with a sense of righteous indignation.

One indication that you're entering the management environment of an Attacker is that it's extremely quiet. Once they've successfully conquered their underlings, the Attackers' employees stop collaborating. If they talk at all, it's in whispers, and there is never any laughter. The atmosphere is thick with tension, populated by the fearful faces of people who eat lunch at their desks so that they never get in trouble for not being available the moment the Attacker wants them.

*Craig, a senior director, thinks nothing of going ballistic whenever someone disagrees with him. Whether in front of members or staff, he takes criticism personally and escalates disagreement to the status of crisis. Rebellious, retaliatory temper tantrums rival Washington's most spectacular 4th of July fireworks displays. When recipients of his attacks, whether for purposes of politics or posterity, become conciliatory, he remains unapproachable, entrenched in his anger, making clear that relationships are irreparably damaged and that no apology will be sufficiently restorative.*

Whether or not you have encountered someone like Craig in your workplace, know this: Such individuals exist in organizational America, are retained by organizational America, and are permitted to exhibit Attacker behaviors with sufficient impunity to imply consent at the highest levels. Indeed, Attackers often occupy the uppermost positions in organizations. The business results they generate make them virtually untouchable, despite the litigious nature of their behaviors. Perhaps they bring in the most revenue or have star quality in the marketplace; perhaps they're friends with the board chair or are responsible for bringing the organization back from the brink of ruin. Whatever the reason, terminating the Attacker is viewed as having more severely negative consequences than suffering whatever financial penalties would ensue from hostile work environment litigation.

When you complain to the brass about the Attacker in your workplace, expect to see shock and horror on their faces as they express sympathy for you; expect to feel cared for and understood as they articulate concern for you; expect to feel validated as they assure you of their desire to retain you. Just don't expect action.

Herculean efforts will be made to placate, coddle, and soothe you. But it's highly unlikely that any punitive action will be taken against the Attacker. Like it or not, agree with it or not, whatever results the Attacker is generating are imbued with greater value than your continued employment, and the consequence of losing the Attacker is seen as a greater risk than your lawsuit.

So how do these folks get into positions of power in the first place? Keep in mind that the abominable behaviors of Attackers aren't linked to intellectual deficiency. They aren't stupid. Without justifying or mitigating their detestable treatment of others, they have utility in society, in organizations, and—believe it or not—in your professional development. Lest you rail against such a statement, consider the following ways in which the Attacker might be useful:

- As a sounding board for your important presentations, revealing any flaws that may exist
- As the person who can handle serious hits from key stakeholders when the organization makes controversial decisions
- As an advocate if you're falsely accused or if you're the victim of some form of discrimination
- As a source of emotional strength and resilience when you're just plain scared

Bottom line, as devil's advocates who prepare you for the worst or foxhole buddies who fight with you through the worst, no one outperforms Attackers. If the Attacker is on your side, you couldn't have a stronger ally or one who is more terrifying to your adversary.

Realizing that others are likely to complain about their abrasiveness, Attackers are careful not to display their abusive behaviors until they have become indispensable at work. Until then, Attackers vent their displeasure everywhere else they can. They'll burst out at the grocery store clerk for slow scanning or for chatting too long with a customer; they'll heave impatient sighs at the dry-cleaning clerk for not being quick enough; they'll spew their poison at anyone whose performance isn't what they think it should be. The pattern is easily discernable. They demonstrate their animosity only toward those who are less powerful, who cannot impose consequences, and with whom they can remain anonymous. Attackers would rather shift their patronage to alternate vendors than deprive themselves of the highly gratifying experience of delivering a blistering tirade to defenseless, low-wage employees.

## Greatest Strengths

Transitioning from the above description to a discussion of the Attacker's strengths may require a considerable effort on your part. Without any intent to glorify the Attackers, to justify or mitigate their detestable treatment of others, it's important to observe their strengths. Additional context is provided here to help establish your receptivity to the idea that even Attackers have strengths.

*The 1965 movie* King Rat *chronicles the experiences of U.S. soldiers in a World War II Japanese POW camp. Somehow the men found a stray dog; it became a beloved mascot. The ranking U.S officer, played by George Segal, killed the dog, cooked it, and ate it with his men before telling them he had done so. He appeared to collude with the enemy, to the point where the Japanese put George in a separate fenced-in area to protect him from his fellow soldiers. He sneered his men, derided them, made fun of their patriotism, and otherwise elicited from them such hatred that, had he been within arms' reach of them, they'd have torn him to shreds. At the end of the movie, on liberation day, all of George's troops are in a covered truck, and George is by himself in another. His men are yelling, screaming, and spitting threats at him, promising to pursue his court martial with religious fervor. In the final moments of the movie, the camera zooms in on George's face, and the viewer realizes that George did all this on purpose. He deliberately made his men hate him, knowing that their hatred would keep them alive.*

Here's the point. Attackers can endure professional loneliness much longer than the rest of us. They can be surrounded by the hatred of others for protracted periods with no need for relief and without ill effect. This strength enables them to make and implement the tough decisions with which no one else wants to be associated. Without losing a wink of sleep, Attackers can lay off thousands of middle managers to accommodate budget cuts; they can announce with pitiless resolve that salaries are being slashed or that benefits are being cut so the organization can survive. Highly resilient and emotionally inviolate, Attackers are among the handful of people who can be eviscerated in the public domain and be invigorated by it.

## Greatest Need

Perhaps surprisingly, Attackers' greatest need is for respect. They grew up at such a deficit of respect that they're willing to use all the tools at their disposal, including fear and intimidation if necessary, to force others to show respect.

They don't care if you like them. They're not out to win any popularity contests. Indeed, they prefer the dislike of others to the revolting alternative of being forced to endure feigned pleasure in relationships.

## Decision Method

Akin to the Commander's decision method of "Do what I say, the way I say, right now," the Attacker modifies this approach to include hostility: "Do exactly what I tell you, right now, and get OUT!"

## Reaction to Feedback

When under attack, Attackers counterattack. They associate direct criticism with disrespect and are retaliatory. The inappropriateness of choosing not to control their verbal output doesn't even make it onto their radar screens. To an Attacker, disagreement isn't about who's right; it's about who will prevail. And more than likely, no matter how powerfully you state your case, no matter how right you are, if you're a peer or a subordinate, the Attacker will overpower you.

Rather than directly reprimanding Attackers, try the more sophisticated technique of using self-convicting questions. Here's how it works. In meetings where multiple people are present, engineer the conversation so that you can ask the Attacker's opinion on excellence in leadership, or collaborative teamwork, or employee relations, whatever the issue. (Monitor your tone of voice; don't sound as if you're baiting the Attacker.) For example: What do you think are the most important characteristics for good leadership? What are your ideas on effectively motivating others? How can you help me put the heart back into this organization? What kinds of management attitudes and behaviors cripple staff drive to succeed? What's the best way to get staff to want to help implement our strategic plan?

Once Attackers respond to such questions, the impact of their usual behavior becomes clearer to them. They become more likely to behave in ways that are consistent with their answers, since doing otherwise would impugn their credibility and earn disrespect. Self-convicting questions are effective with Attackers because in asking their opinions, you're showing respect and because in answering your questions, they're setting the bar for their own performance.

**Now go to the Predictive Grid on page 15 and enter a score from 5 to 25 in column B, indicating the degree to which you fit the Attacker description.**

## Managing Vulnerability to the Attacker Superior

Because the Attackers' attacks are often personal in nature (Your upbringing must have been lacking; your alma mater gave you passing grades to meet a quota; whoever hired you was an imbecile.), they can be tantamount to verbal abuse. If you're a pretty tough cookie, your natural outrage can cause an adrenaline rush that makes you want to leap to your own defense, and that's exactly how Attacker bosses make you vulnerable. They push you to the point that you lose your composure, sink to their level, and engage in retaliatory behavior. Doing so, however, will only elicit intensified abuse from the Attacker. Managing your vulnerability in such situations will require that you realize the futility of attempting to reason with Attackers and that you adopt android-like response patterns.

If you're not such a tough cookie, the constant barrage of verbal onslaughts from the Attacker can crush your spirit. Your emotional tenderness will be exploited by the Attacker boss. Echoes of painful comments can bring you to tears in the middle of the night and cause continuing pain for years to come. Reducing your vulnerability will require that you minimize the damage to yourself, which means you have to get out from under the Attacker boss. If you know you're not wired to cope with Attacker behavior, transfer or quit, but get out! Don't wait for someone to come along and save you from the Attacker. Act to save yourself.

## Adapting Techniques for Interacting With Attacker Superiors

Your objective cannot be to change the Attacker. Instead, your challenge is to neutralize the Attacker's negative impacts on yourself and others while getting the business results you need.

- **Don't take the Attacker's attacks personally** and become offended. Understand that it's not you; they detest everyone equally!

- **Listen only for the facts,** and hit your mental delete button on every personal insult the Attacker levies. Strive to ignore the belittling commentary.

- **Focus on delivering results.** Accept that working successfully with Attackers requires a highly disciplined focus on results, ignoring all else.

- **Set aside your righteous indignation** and stay focused on the business results you need. Is it okay for them to be personal with their criticism? Of course not. Is it appropriate for them to speak to you the way they do? Of course not. Can you go to HR and complain? Of course you can. Can you sue them? Probably. Would this make you more effective in interacting with the Attacker? No. Does that mean you should let Attackers wipe their feet on you? No! But reacting to an Attacker's behavior will just make it worse, and you won't get the results you need. So stay focused on results, not on your feelings.

- **Look for opportunities to show respect.** Select from among the Attacker's repertoire of achievements, and ask specific questions about these. When time proves the Attacker right about something that was controversial, acknowledge it. Try saying "You were right; I was wrong; what did you see that I didn't?"

- **Buffer others.** If you know you're tough enough to work successfully with Attackers, consider setting yourself up as a buffer between the Attacker and his or her other subordinates or peers. Your ability to work successfully with Attackers will distinguish you among others who either can't or don't want to do so.

- **Don't get emotional.** Try to adopt and maintain android-like behavior.

- **Minimize time with the Attacker.** Expedite interactions to preserve your emotional safety.

- **Let them vent.** Be a good listener, and let them exhaust their aggravation. When Attackers are particularly irritated, ask questions that elicit continued venting. Be a good listener, and let them spew their venom until they're purged.

- **Monitor your intonation,** facial expressions, and body behavior to edit out signs of exasperation or disrespect.

- **Be prepared for the devil's advocate** when you deal with the Attacker. Expect that any work product you take into the Attacker's office will be ripped to shreds. Yes, it's going to hurt, but pay attention to the substance of the criticisms; you'll learn how to enhance your own critical assessment skills.

- **Use humor to disarm the Attacker.** Humor is the weapon of the angels, and can be effective in disarming Attackers. But be careful. If you aren't naturally funny, don't try to be humorous with the Attacker and never use humor at his or her expense.

- **Don't get into arguments with Attackers.** Don't let their behaviors take you hostage, reducing you to their level.

## Managing Vulnerability to the Attacker Subordinate

As subordinates, Attackers devastate the morale of the rest of your staff. They cripple teamwork and, to the extent they are known as Attackers by those outside your department, they damage your reputation as a manager. Assuming you're aware that an Attacker subordinate is among your direct reports, your first priority is to protect your other subordinates, since they are more likely to suffer at the hands of the Attacker than you are. Your second priority is to conduct a careful cost/benefit analysis of retaining your Attacker subordinate. It may not be worth the time you'll have to spend smoothing the ruffled feathers of those with whom the Attacker interacts. If you determine that pruning out the Attacker isn't the right decision, the management tips that follow will prove helpful.

## Adapting Techniques for Interacting With Attacker Subordinates

Remember, Attackers aren't likely to demonstrate their hostile behavior in front of their bosses. Instituting peer reviews or 360-degree reviews will help reveal the presence of Attackers on your staff.

- **Counsel your other subordinates** to help them cope effectively with the Attacker in their midst.

- **Reroute workflow to minimize interactions** between your Attacker subordinate and all others.

- **Consider carefully before assigning staff to your Attacker** subordinate. Generally, Attackers are hurtful managers and shouldn't be allowed to manage others.

- **Consider how you might better isolate your Attacker** subordinate. Perhaps there is a rationale to justify working from home.

- **Link the Attacker's career progression** to the absence of inflammatory behavior.

- **Consider retaining a coach** for your Attacker subordinates.

- **Informally mentor your Attacker** subordinate. Assign selected readings to be discussed when you meet. The case studies found in the first 100 pages of *Working with Emotional Intelligence* by Daniel Goleman (Bantam Books, 1998) are a great resource for this purpose.

- **Consider carefully what work** the organization can offer that may align better with the strengths of your Attacker subordinate.
- **Recommend a strenuous exercise regimen** to help your Attacker subordinate reduce and manage stress.

## Other Styles Attackers Find Most Challenging:
- Drifters, for their seeming unflappability
- Pleasers, for the contemptuous sin of caring about people
- Avoiders, for what Attackers see as their spinelessness

## Actual 360-Degree Input on Attackers

Attackers are, at all times, aggravated by people. Even more important than being valued and validated for doing what the rest of us think of as the really hard things, they want to be acknowledged for having the mettle to endure others. The 360-degree input on Attackers discloses the wounded feelings they cause in others.

### Here's what their superiors have to say:
- *Won't engage with others who haven't earned her respect, with those who aren't considered by her to be intellectual equals. This creates hostility.*
- *Is gruff, unpolished; seems to take disagreements personally, becoming snippy.*
- *Becomes visibly annoyed and impatient when others don't convey their thoughts as he thinks they should.*
- *Undervalues the intelligence and ideas of others. Irritable, caustic, and proud of it.*
- *We've spent a great deal of time trying to make him productive and professional. He has caused great damage to the association on all levels, including morale, dollars expended, and services to membership.*
- *Rather than providing the valuable dissenting voice, she is chronically demotivating.*

### Here's what their peers have to say:
- *Drills people in public, battering them with accusatory questions when clearly, the interaction should be private.*
- *She screams at her boss, her peers, her subordinates. It's shocking. Such outrageous disrespect and lack of control on her part is astonishing to witness.*
- *Has a short fuse. Is extremely confrontational and combative. Malicious, insulting, condescending, even volatile. Alienates others.*

- *I have seen grown men quake as they debate about whether to consult her on a minor decision or risk making the decision themselves.*

- *Out-shouts anyone who disagrees. Is rude and immature. Is oblivious to the sensitivities of individuals. Hopeless to try to get through.*

- *Makes snide comments to us about one another. Pits people against each other.*

## Here's what their subordinates have to say:

- *Unbearable. Spiteful and mean. Dreadful to work with. Caustic and divisive.*

- *Treats people like dirt. Barks out orders as if we're slaves. Is self-righteous and discourteous. Arrogant and crass.*

- *Slams doors, yells, curses, is always frightening and sometimes terrifying. Has thrown papers across the room, while screaming at staff. Actually uses the word "forbid."*

- *He focuses exclusively on what we do wrong and how we disappoint him. His behavior creates a sense of futility. Deflated, disenfranchised, and marginalized, we know we can never satisfy him.*

- *When I speak up, it's because I care. But if I speak up, she'll take my head off. So, I have two choices: speak up and be eviscerated by her or don't speak up and be disrespected by her. Guess I have to learn not to care about my work.*

- *Our senior director rules by intimidation. He puts everyone in fear for their jobs, and blames others for everything. His management diminishes others. We're learning how NOT to manage.*

# CHAPTER 5

# The Pleaser

| | |
|---|---|
| SWEET, KIND | THOUGHTFUL |
| HIGH SOCIAL NEEDS | WITHHOLDS BAD NEWS |
| REASSURING | AGREEABLE |
| DEFERENTIAL | SYMPATHETIC |
| EASY TO GET ALONG WITH | NEEDS EVERYONE TO AGREE |
| PLACATING, GIVES IN EASILY | WON'T CRITICIZE |
| WON'T CONFRONT PROBLEMS | LIKES PERSONAL APPROACH |
| DISABLED BY CONFLICT OR ANGER | NEEDS APPROVAL |

*W*ELL KNOWN AS ONE WHO WOULD *bend over backward to suit anyone's agenda or to soothe anyone's ruffled feathers, the CEO, Bernard, routinely made decisions that allowed him the luxury of sidestepping conflict and delaying, sometimes perpetually, more difficult decisions. Because his entire exec team knew how to "play him" and because he gives nothing but succor to those involved in a dispute, the futility of going to him for the tough decisions or other issues requiring strong leadership was common knowledge. The result was anarchy within the ranks. Because each senior exec could act with impunity, each implemented his or her own agenda without regard for impact on peers. Each was powerless to reign in the other, and many resorted to retaliatory acts, including upstaging of one another, withholding of crucial information, and blatant noncompliance with requirements. Needing everyone to like him, this CEO didn't even make an attempt to exhibit anything even remotely akin to strong leadership. Believing that his benevolent caring for others would serve as a template for his direct reports to emulate, he imputed the best to his execs, and incorrectly assumed they were getting along, when in fact, Armageddon was playing out below his radar screen.*

Bernard's behavior typifies Pleasers' view of workplace associates as extended family. Their need to take care of others produces exaggerated socialization at the office, so they check in with others at the water fountain, in the lavatory, at the coffee machines, and in the kitchenette. They spend a tremendous amount of time on the telephone and in person being sympathetic and reassuring. They listen attentively, and respond with soothing coos, consoling pats, and whenever possible, encouraging hugs. They're often so busy taking care of their workplace family, fussing over all their little chicks, that they don't get their own work done during the normal business day. To the Pleaser, the number-one priority is to be available for others, no matter what's needed.

Thin-skinned and tenderhearted, Pleasers are pleasant, caring, and friendly. Their personal warmth is augmented by thoughtful actions, kind words, and an agreeable nature. Although the congenial disposition of Pleasers makes them seem easy to get along with, they can be extremely high-maintenance employees.

With a high need for inclusion, Pleasers like to be part of meetings, activities, and your life. Their feelings can be hurt when they are excluded. They self-actualize by helping others. So if you don't say "good morning" as soon as you walk in the office, they're tugging at your cuffs wanting to know what's wrong so they can make it better or be helpful. Pregnant pauses, soulful looks, and seemingly hurt feelings are perceptible if you don't confide in the Pleaser. If nothing is wrong or if you just don't want to discuss it, you may need to fabricate something minor just to get the Pleaser to leave you alone.

*Characterized as being overly sensitive and high maintenance, Director Saundra was reputed to lack intelligence because she was so accommodating and deferential. Her selflessness led to her contributions being not just overlooked, but unknown. Faced with the fact that her own behaviors resulted in her work being marginalized and unappreciated, this director had no idea how to set things right. Without the emotional resilience needed to cope effectively with being diminished by others, Saundra felt the only solution was to start fresh somewhere else.*

Unable to say no to others regardless of the cost to themselves, Pleasers are always willing to take on extra work. No matter the volume of requests, no matter how frequent the requests, even if they're being taken advantage of, as in Saundra's case, Pleasers just keep on doing for others. To them, the word *no* connotes rejection and personal failure and results in their being disliked.

In combination with the productivity losses attendant to their highly social personality, the inability to say no often results in lots of extra hours for the Pleaser. Not wanting to disappoint anyone by missing deadlines, Pleasers will do whatever it takes to get the job done. They'll work evenings and weekends, and you'll never know because they'll never tell you. Pleasers don't play a martyr's role. They'll just pay whatever price has to be paid to please everyone. As a result, Pleasers are perpetually flirting with emotional and physical burnout. Well-intentioned warnings from others about this danger go unheeded because Pleasers just can't make themselves stop helping. They'll keep at it until they finally burn out.

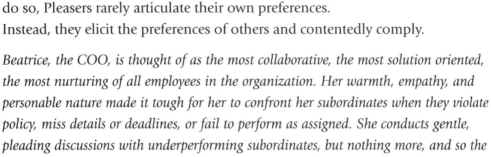

Because Pleasers really believe that your wants and needs truly are more important than their own, they're extremely deferential. Quick to give in and happy to do so, Pleasers rarely articulate their own preferences. Instead, they elicit the preferences of others and contentedly comply.

*Beatrice, the COO, is thought of as the most collaborative, the most solution oriented, the most nurturing of all employees in the organization. Her warmth, empathy, and personable nature made it tough for her to confront her subordinates when they violate policy, miss details or deadlines, or fail to perform as assigned. She conducts gentle, pleading discussions with underperforming subordinates, but nothing more, and so the problems continue. Even when peers in other departments complain to her about the inadequate deliverables of her subordinates, Beatrice imposes no further consequences.*

Physiologically disabled by interpersonal stress, Pleasers like Beatrice may develop migraines, nosebleeds, or stomach problems when involved in conflicts. Pleasers won't be able to choose between a spouse who wants them to go out to dinner and the boss who wants them to work late because the competing needs would require disappointing one or the other. Their bodies resolve the dilemma for them by producing real physical distress.

*Despite long-term blatant insubordination, colossal failures in service deliveries, and extreme emotional immaturity, a director is now entering her 10th year with the organization. Reason? The CEO, Ruth, is unwilling to take appropriate disciplinary action. The whole organization knows that those with long tenure are protected by the CEO who repeatedly demonstrates a loathing to confront poor performance. Even more disheartening than the negative impact on morale is the cost imposed on the organization by accepting the mediocre business outcomes produced by the director.*

The need for a tranquil work environment prevents Pleasers like Ruth from criticizing or confronting others. They won't ask the tough questions, won't stand up for themselves or complain even when they've been badly treated, and won't take a hard line with others, even when doing so would be justified. Instead, they say only what others want to hear. This need for peace and harmony can be so pronounced that Pleasers may be disqualified for job duties that involve negotiation, discipline, rejection, disappointment, or candid assessment.

As gracious and amenable as Pleasers are, they can create real havoc in the workplace. For example, a 64-year-old secretary who had endured multiple back surgeries decided to brave a major snow storm to take completed work to her employer's home. During the journey, her vehicle got stuck in the snow, so she abandoned it and walked the remaining two miles. She then trudged up a long, steep driveway and, radiant with a tremendous sense of purpose, delivered work for which there was no deadline. Why would she make such a foolish and potentially dangerous decision? Not to meet a deadline, not to earn a promotion or a reward of any kind. She did it to show devotion. Had her employer chastised her as being reckless and ridiculous, she would have been heartbroken. Her objective was to demonstrate commitment and caring, which if trivialized or diminished, would have been deeply wounding.

But what if, after braving the winter weather and trudging through more than three feet of snow despite her age and without regard for her back problems, she beams happily at her employer and hands in documents that, with only a cursory overview, reveal multiple errors? Such acts of devotion are typical of Pleasers, and these acts tend to hold us hostage when we need to provide critical feedback. In this case, if possible, the employer should first see to the comfort of the employee, spend time talking about the brave feat she just accomplished, and segue slowly into a review of the document.

Here's another example. A Pleaser is the receptionist whose best friend at the office has decided to slip out for the rest of the day. The friend leaves her computer on, leaves her jacket on her chair, and places an empty purse at her workstation. She walks through the reception area and asks her Pleaser friend to cover for her. Inevitably, the boss comes looking for the Pleaser's friend, but the Pleaser won't reveal the deception. With unintentional disregard for the radial impacts on the organization, the Pleaser is concerned only about making sure that no one gets upset with her. If she convincingly denies all knowledge, neither her friend nor her employer can be mad at her. Such misplaced priorities are typical of Pleasers; they subordinate what's best for the organization to the maintenance of relationships.

## Greatest Strengths

With their comforting, supportive, collaborative behavior, Pleasers humanize the workplace. They lift us up when we're down, give compliments that always align with what we most want to be recognized for, and create a sense of belonging by paying attention to the small things. They know the names of our family members, remember the special occasions in our lives, and make us feel cared for.

Pleasers personify safe harbors where acceptance seems unconditional and where solace and succor are available for our bruised and battered feelings. Indeed, they may be the only people in our lives who don't seem to have expectations of us. Always ready with mitigating perspectives, they help us cope not only with the thoughtless acts of others but with ourselves as well.

## Greatest Need

The greatest need of Pleasers is to be liked and accepted by everyone. Perpetual affirmation of others' regard is of primary importance.

## Decision Method

Pleasers make whatever decisions will ensure they continue to be liked by others. They are miscast when required to make controversial decisions and are ill equipped to make tough choices that may be divisive. Prioritizing relationships over what's best for the organization is an easy choice for Pleasers.

## Reaction to Feedback

Not surprisingly, the tender-hearted Pleaser is often emotionally overwhelmed by negative feedback and can't control the tears. Because your approval is so important to them, they will feign agreement with your criticisms rather than engage in a substantive discussion of the issues.

*Gretta, a contract provider of secretarial services, consistently provides services above and beyond what she invoices. She enjoys seeing the delighted surprise in her client's faces when she delivers unexpected value. However, her work is frequently late, and this tardiness creates considerable difficulties for clients with significant deadlines. When they express their chagrin, Gretta feels deeply wounded.*

It's easy to imagine that Gretta's client would be tempted to apologize, even though the expectation of timeliness was reasonable, simply because Gretta was so hurt. Because tears are so frequently a component of the Pleaser's response to feedback, this four-step no-more-tears formula should prove especially useful. First, give the Pleaser your written feedback a day or two before you want to discuss it. This gives the Pleaser a chance to exhaust the tears before meeting with you. Second, once the meeting is in progress, the moment tears begin, calmly stop the meeting and take a five-minute break, during which time the Pleaser must leave your office. Even if the Pleaser assures you he or she is all right and requests that the meeting proceed, insist that the Pleaser leave your office for a short break. Third, resume the meeting, and if the tears begin again, reschedule the meeting for the next day, gently stressing that, no matter what, the meeting will proceed to its conclusion at that time. Even if you have to do this over the objections of the Pleaser, it's important at this point to take an overnight break. Finally, if the tears begin again during the rescheduled meeting, you can pass the tissues, but otherwise ignore them and press on.

In combination, these techniques imply the expectation of professional behavior without being critical and maximize the opportunity for the Pleaser to regain and maintain composure. This process also demonstrates that emotionalism is insufficient as a deterrent to the provision of performance feedback.

Another effective tool for providing day-to-day feedback to the Pleaser is the sandwich technique, which requires any critical observation to be sandwiched between two phrases of praise. For example: "I very much appreciate your tact and diplomacy in dealing with our vendors; you're really good at communicating what's required without being dictatorial. However, you're failing to include in those communications the various ways in which we'll be measuring their performance. Their success, and ours, depends on the clarity of and compliance with all relevant measures. I know that I can rely on your outstanding interpersonal skills and your knowledge of the performance requirements to ensure our vendor communications are complete."

**Now go to the Predictive Grid on page 15 and enter a score from 5 to 25 in column B, indicating the degree to which you fit the Pleaser description.**

## Managing Vulnerability to the Pleaser Superior

As bosses, Pleasers won't give you the critical feedback you need to grow and develop. At performance review time, they won't have any complaints, and if they do, the phraseology will be so tactful as to escape recognition. In emotionally charged cases, Pleasers may ask their own boss or an HR executive to address a tough issue, while taking on the role of silent observer. Accept that it's useless to attempt to persuade Pleasers to say anything negative about you. Repeated petitions for constructive criticism will elicit only further affirmations or vagaries. Leverage your vulnerability here by soliciting feedback from other relevant internal colleagues, including, as appropriate, internal customers and suppliers, peers, subordinates, or other department personnel with whom you collaborate.

## Adapting Techniques for Interacting With Pleaser Superiors

- **Don't expect umpiring.** Recognize that your Pleaser boss isn't likely to help you resolve conflicts. Stop beating your head against the wall expecting him or her to do so. You'll have to step up and resolve your own difficulties or go to someone else for help.

- **Elicit what's hidden by tact.** Pleaser superiors are notoriously inexplicit when it comes to making unpopular decisions or assignments. As a result, your clarifying questions must be particularly explicit. Alternatively, you can offer to act in their stead, so you're the one taking the heat.

- **Equip your boss to confront poor performance.** Pleaser superiors routinely fail to impose accountability for poor performance. To the extent you have line-of-sight into the suboptimal performance of those reporting to your Pleaser boss, you can draft a few relevant sentences your boss can use to address performance issues.

- **Be upbeat.** Pleasers are sensitive to their environments. Don't be a complainer. Edit out of conversations with the Pleaser any tendency to be cranky or negative. Instead, work to consistently emphasize the positive.

- **Spend time with the people who interact with the Pleaser.** Getting to know their world imbues you with the credibility necessary for the Pleaser to trust your advice.

- **Emphasize commonalities, agreement, and unity.** Rather than pointing out the chasms that may exist between and among people or departments, make references to shared experiences, similar values, and characteristics to help the Pleaser navigate the tough times.

- **As often as you can, offer to help** the Pleaser. Actively seek opportunities to work alongside the Pleaser and pitch in or to provide words of encouragement.

## Managing Vulnerability to the Pleaser Subordinate

As your subordinates, Pleasers make you vulnerable by withholding the bad news you need to manage effectively. They won't inform you about something that will get someone else in trouble; instead, they'll feign ignorance to protect others. Without malice or ill intent, they'll lie to you about something they know would upset you in order to buy themselves time to fix it so that you never even know it happened in the first place.

To leverage this vulnerability, you'll need to continually stress the concept of the greater good. Begin doing so now, preemptively, so that the concept becomes a consideration in the Pleaser's mind the next time a choice is being made to supply or withhold information. If Pleasers understand that by protecting one person they put numerous others at risk, they are more likely to keep you informed.

## Adapting Techniques for Interacting With Pleaser Subordinates

- **Use a familial approach.** Know the names and significant activities of the Pleaser's family members; acknowledge significant dates and events. Make a big deal about the little things in the Pleaser's life.

- **Take a personal interest** in Pleasers as individuals. Ask for their opinions and advice. Inquire about their feelings, health, and projects.

- **Facilitate receptivity.** Collaborate with the Pleaser on how tough messages could best be communicated. Articulate a concern that the message be well received by those affected. Engage the Pleaser in brainstorming how to ensure others' receptivity.

- **Acknowledge Pleasers' fiduciary behavior.** Pleasers have a concern for thoroughness in checking contracts, references, and warranties, and they manifest a protective posture toward outsiders regarding their work family. They want you to know how much they care, and when you acknowledge them for these behaviors, it reveals your awareness of their caring.

- **Help the Pleaser learn to say no** without having to use the word *no*. Encourage a Pleaser to keep a current list of output obligations, including deadlines and customer names, and require each new petitioner to conduct whatever negotiations are necessary to secure inclusion of their task on the Pleaser's list. This way, the Pleaser can express a willingness to do the work without actually accepting it. Or they could explain that they're no longer allowed to take on any work that hasn't first been approved by the boss. This way, it's not the Pleaser but the Pleaser's boss who's the bad guy.

- **Demonstrate esteem for the Pleaser's belief** that people are more important than data, money, or things. Even if you don't share this belief, assure Pleasers that their perspective helps rein you in when you're being too gruff.

- **Don't communicate with Pleasers when you're angry.** They're discomfited by anger, even if it isn't directed at them. Wait until you can converse calmly and quietly.

- **Identify or create opportunities for the Pleaser to help** others. Pleasers derive their greatest satisfaction by helping others and consider it a gift when you craft additional opportunities for them to do so.

- **Don't leap immediately to business** when initiating interaction with the Pleaser, and don't rush through the interaction, failing to give the Pleaser a chance to ask questions. Instead, take a few moments to break the ice with a personal comment or question.

- **Send greeting cards**—thank-you cards, birthday cards, holiday cards, get well cards, "just because" cards.

- **Look for opportunities to include the Pleaser** in groups, initiatives, and activities.

## Other Styles Pleasers Find Most Challenging:
- Commanders, because of their unwillingness to establish a relationship
- Attackers, because of their deliberate hostility toward others
- Analyticals, since the Pleaser can never seem to satisfy them or gain their trust

## Actual 360-Degree Input on Pleasers

Pleasers want to be valued and validated for their compassionate, helpful natures. Although most of us would claim to view these as desirable traits, prolonged interaction with those whose primary need is to be liked can evoke a contradictory assessment, as revealed in this 360–degree input about Pleasers.

### Here's what their superiors have to say:

- *Spends more time trying to keep people happy than getting the job done.*

- *Elevates emotion (hers and others') to the point that business results are impeded.*

- *Manages around poor performers rather than eliminating them. If they turn in unacceptable work, she fixes it. If they ignore directives, she takes no action.*

- *Unwilling to be the "heavy." Won't give people the news they don't want to hear but need to hear.*

- *He has far too many direct reports because he won't upset people by changing their reporting relationship.*

- *Is very focused on people's feelings and lets this override getting the job done.*

### Here's what their peers have to say:

- *Allows herself to be handcuffed; won't push back when she should. Obsesses about relationships to the point of seeming insecure.*

- *On an endless salvage mission; won't terminate underperforming employees. Works around their weaknesses and makes excuses for them to avoid hurt feelings.*

- *He knowingly allowed a divisive, poisonous, hateful employee who did untold damage to stay here for years, merely because he couldn't bring himself to terminate her.*

- *Promotes anyone who threatens to leave just to keep them happy. Creates new positions, new levels in the hierarchy, for anyone who whines or threatens to leave.*

- *If it's uncomfortable or distasteful, he won't deal with it. Requires subordinates to resolve conflicts that occur outside their own areas so he can avoid dealing with it, even when the difficulty has escalated beyond their scope.*

- *She agrees to whatever anyone wants, so we function in a constant state of crisis. She's trying to be everything to everyone so no one is disappointed. This is an impossible situation.*

**Here's what their subordinates have to say:**

- *I'm usually left wondering what the message really is. Negative feedback is so softly stated that I can't understand the message. It's as if he's trying to be a buddy instead of a boss.*

- *Tolerating poor or marginal employees destroys our morale. When we complain about this to our boss, she empathizes and says she understands, but never takes action. We've given up hoping she'll make the tough decisions.*

- *Anyone who knows how to tell a good sob story can get away with anything.*

- *Employees who perpetually make mistakes have solid job security. They are never confronted, and never held accountable, so they have no motivation to change their ways. This holds true even for vendors who repeatedly fail to perform.*

- *He erodes our esteem for the bonus plan because he goes to bat for anyone who doesn't meet the criteria. This renders "making it" meaningless.*

- *Two of us were continually tripping over each other, being redundant and inefficient, because our boss didn't want to hurt our feelings by clarifying who would keep what and who would lose what.*

# CHAPTER 6

# The Performer

FLASHY

SELF-PROMOTER

FAST RATE OF SPEECH

OVER COMMITTED

NARCISSISTIC

IN A HURRY

SHOW-OFF

OVERPRAISES OTHERS

FLAMBOYANT

NEEDS CONSTANT ATTENTION

TALKATIVE

STATUS CONSCIOUS

JOVIAL, LOUD

MANIPULATIVE

SELF-SERVING

FUN TO BE AROUND

*S*TEPHAN, THE HEAD OF INDUSTRY AFFAIRS, *was racking up success after success on the Hill. In addition to these high-profile outcomes, however, his goals and objectives for the year required that he become more compliant with policies and procedures and more collaborative with peers. His Hill successes, he claimed at review time, would not have been possible had he deigned to deliver on his other goals and objectives.*

Funny, engaging, jovial, and entertaining, Performers are often the favorite personality in the workplace. Their wit and mental quickness make people laugh. Their humor charms, delights, and uplifts everyone; they're a breath of fresh air, and others enjoy being around them. In any gathering, just look for a laughing crowd; in its midst will be the Performer. And you can continue to enjoy and delight in the Performer—as did Stephan's colleagues—until you have to rely on him or her for something.

Performers' interest in and effort toward any initiative is directly linked to the possibility of stardom. If there is runway potential, they will be highly motivated and will likely far exceed expectations. Otherwise, they'll offload their responsibilities to the person they've already primed to receive them. This person is the one with whom the Performer shares confidential information, the one for whom the Performer uses his or her connections to secure preferential treatment

and special opportunities, the one who the Performer somehow features to the organization as being exceptional. In return, this individual is always at the ready, virtually panting to absorb whatever tasks the Performer wants to shed and taking care of all the pesky details so loathed by the Performer.

*Mark, the longtime director of the department that brought in the bulk of nondues revenue, considers himself exempt from all the rules others have to follow. He consistently violates agreements, thumbs his nose at policy, disregards reporting requirements, and ignores internal emails. He does all this with an attitude of arrogance, almost daring anyone to complain, because he's convinced that he's untouchable. Always functioning outside the bounds, Mark sometimes goes so far that he simply must be confronted. On these occasions, he's apologetic and promises to do better, but this proves to be merely lip service. He behaves only for a week or two before reverting to his usual lack of compliance.*

Mark's behavior provides a perfect example of how Performers overpromise when it looks good, and underdeliver when it counts. In venues where it's smart to do so, they'll put their hands up and step forward, volunteering for the unpopular projects that no one else wants to do. With the perfect blend of humility and humor, they endear themselves to others by setting the example of selflessness and service. Then when it comes time to make good on their pledge, in tones that convince you they're truly distraught and desolated, Performers explain that they've been victimized by the organization, that additional responsibilities have been thrust on them so that they are no longer in a position to deliver. With seemingly heartfelt frustration in their voices, they actually elicit your sympathy as they explain how valiantly they fought to keep ownership of whatever it was they promised to do. You end up really feeling their emotional anguish, even though they reneged.

Performers are self-promoting hustlers and masters of illusion. Great dates and lousy spouses, lots of sizzle but no steak, Performers are masters of their art form: all talk and no action. Because it creates the perception that they're hard workers, Performers are usually among those who arrive at work very early. Their first order of business is to visit others who come in early and regale them with stories about what they've done recently to help another employee; what they've done for various civic groups and charities; how they saved the organization from ruin, impressed the board, got a standing ovation at a speech, or continually give up their personal time for the betterment of the organization, despite the absence of appreciation, which they repeatedly say is not what they want. By this time, employees are arriving in other departments, and the Performer is off to begin all over again with this new group, and another, and another. No one objects, because Performer monologues are always entertaining. When someone from the Performer's own department expresses exasperation at not having been able to locate him or her, the Performer feigns surprise and with baffled indignation claims to have been in meetings all morning.

Performers send emails very late at night, are often required to be at off-site consultations, and are always sprinting from one seemingly important meeting to the next. As a result, Performers are often seen only in profile by those who are awaiting outcomes from them. As they speed through the day at drag-race pace, Performers rarely have time to update their internal customers on work in progress. Fast walking, fast talking, constant rushing, late night messages, and numerous meetings all combine to create the perception of an extremely busy, very important person—which is exactly the perception the Performer wants everyone to have. In truth, the Performer's activity merely masquerades as productivity. Performers are so busy running around promoting themselves that they aren't getting the work done. Although a massive amount of work may be undertaken by the Performer's subordinates, very little is actually being produced by the Performer.

Yet another advantage to their breathless pace is the built-in mitigation it provides for any failure to communicate on their part. They use their rushing as a tactic to insulate themselves from accountability. Here's how it works:

- If you asked for something and they didn't deliver, they can claim that because they were rushing to do something very important, they must have misunderstood you. Because you remember that they were indeed rushing, this seems a plausible defense.

- If you complain that the Performer hasn't updated you, the Performer can claim otherwise, suggesting that because the conversation in which he or she recalls having updated you was on the fly, you may not have retained it. Because you remember the conversation with the Performer was on the fly, this seems a plausible defense.

- If you can't remember the specifics, you certainly can't hold Performers accountable for whatever it was they said they'd do for you—which is, in fact, the plan—because they weren't going to do it anyway.

Reliably unreliable, Performers miss details and deadlines and they fail to follow up. But their flurried, frenetic profusion of activity and their affable manner combine to blur your memory and make you question yourself. You may have walked into the Performer's office with the intent of imposing accountability, but you'll walk out convinced that you're the one who dropped the ball.

Over time, if you're an astute observer, you may come to recognize this crazy-making pattern of behavior for exactly what it is: a false impression of productivity artfully created around high-profile projects to inflate perceptions of their status. Once you're able to discern this pattern, don't delude yourself into thinking you'll be able to convince others of it; they're too enamored of the Performer to believe it.

Protracted periods of aloneness decimate the morale of Performers. From the time they awaken until the time they fall into bed exhausted, they're performing. Everyone—anyone—is an audience. Masters of magnetism, they strike just the right mix of flash and diffidence: sporting embroidered initials on their cuffs one day and wearing jeans the next, stubbornly insisting on a corner office and then initiating substantive conversations about your children, engaging in name dropping as they rush off, and then surprising you with lunch on their return, being a loud and boisterous show-off one minute and disarming you with self-effacing, poignant stories the next.

*Two senior vice presidents, Frank and Gerry, were locked in an endless effort to establish superiority. So shameless were these playground gladiators that they didn't even try to hide their duels from staff. The primary mission of each was to outdo, undo, outshine, and undermine the other, and they engaged in an ever-broadening constituency in their battle to win, involving board members and other external parties in their indiscriminate quest for position and recognition.*

As the story of Frank and Gerry exemplifies, Performers are best suited to the solo role of individual contributors; teams hold no allure for them. Indeed, they don't make good teammates. With an insatiable need to best their peers, they will pay verbal homage to team agreements and then work behind the scenes to siphon off glory for themselves and enhance their own images. In any discussion about team accomplishments, the Performer can't recall others' contributions and bemoans the considerable allowances that had to be made for the alleged youth, inexperience, or lack of expertise of other team members.

Careful to dispel any impression of self-pity, the Performer further capitalizes on this veiled complaint by mentioning how nice it was to mentor needy others and that stepping up to shoulder the lion's share of the workload for the team was actually an enriching experience.

Oozing with ambassadorial sophistication, Performers are charismatic representatives of the organization who excel at establishing relationships—but not at maintaining them. If a disgruntled member needs to be brought back into the fold, the Performer can do it; if the leading company in your industry isn't yet a member, the Performer can snag it; if negotiations are approaching an impasse, the Performer's wit and political acumen will dissolve the tension in an instant. Gifted speakers on an extemporaneous basis, Performers can captivate and sway audiences even amid hostile press. Eloquence and humor delivered on demand from Performers comes at a price, however, and that price is favored status.

Performers are supremely talented at coercing the largest bonus, wheedling inclusion in activities at the highest levels, and justifying the largest empire. If such rewards are withheld, Performers become obsessed with a sense of entitlement. They complain bitterly to everyone, including board members; become divisive as they rally and manipulate their supporters; and drop well-placed hints about plans to resign.

*Tim, one of the senior executives, had the same biological clock, the same work ethic, and the same few family obligations as the CEO, with the result that the two of them often worked together late into the evening and on weekends. Tim flaunted this shared camaraderie with the CEO, lorded it over his peers, and used it to validate or to derail the agendas of others.*

Particularly worthy of note about Performers like Tim is the skill with which they engineer negative consequences for you if you impede them in any way. Whether you actually besmirch their image, prevent them from getting an opportunity to improve their image, or merely reduce the intensity of the spotlight that's shining on them, their retaliatory actions will be effective without being attributable. For example, without saying a single negative word, they can cause your boss to infer that you're not pulling your weight, knit together a series of seemingly disconnected facts or events that coalesce in an unpredictable way to embarrass you, and create indebtedness in others that results in split loyalties. Given the Performer's need for attention, it's ironic that they have no need to display the "Gotcha!" grin. They're content to slither in the background, satisfied in the knowledge that their retaliatory maneuvering was effective.

## Greatest Strengths

Captivating public speakers, Performers are immensely talented in the art of persuasion and at establishing relationships. Their verbal fluency combined with witty self-confidence makes them indispensable in convincing key stakeholders to agree, comply, commit, or change. By the time Performers are done with you, you'd be embarrassed not to come on board and do whatever they want you to do. They seem to have a sixth sense for striking the perfect balance between self-importance and self-effacement, keeping everyone else just off balance enough to give Performers the benefit of the doubt.

## Greatest Need

Be number one! Get the Trophy! Get your name in the paper! Win the tournament! Be the Star! Get the lead role! Such expectations were among the primary messages that formed the developmental context of the Performer. As a result, they come to believe that, absent external validation of their worth, they haven't any.

*Intent on securing accolades from his boss, the board, and the media, Bill, the director of membership, was so starved for attention that in every possible instance he described in detail and with great enthusiasm how he and his department had surpassed expectations. Even when confronted with the acrimony this was causing among his peers, he insisted on keeping others informed of everything he and his department had accomplished. Focused exclusively on achieving favored status, Bill thought it outrageous to request that he show concern for what he considered to be the jealousy and bitterness of others.*

Recognition is the greatest need of Performers. Withholding recognition from Performers or impeding opportunities for it will evoke retaliatory behavior, which, albeit covert, will nonetheless stymie the achievement of available, incremental business gains.

## Decision Method

Performers don't make decisions based on what's best for the organization, what's best for members, or what's best for the team. Instead, Performers reconfigure almost every situation into a deal-making opportunity so that there is always something in it for them. Their decisions are driven by whatever will cast them in the most favorable light.

## Reaction to Feedback

When receiving criticism, Performers have three response modes:

- **Blame someone else** for the failure. "If she had pulled her share of the weight…or if he hadn't done what he did, I would have been able to…."

- **Deny that they ever agreed** to do something in the first place. "I said it was possible, that I'd try; I never said it was definite! I think because I so often create magic, it is becoming expected of me."

- **Rationalize failure** as the inevitable result of unreasonable expectations. "C'mon! No one could have achieved that percentage. The goal was based on faulty assumptions."

When offering Performers critical feedback, communicate your point in an impersonal, noncritical way by using the technique of storytelling. Here's how. Whatever the fault, assign it to a fictional character employed by a different organization and weave into the story sufficient similarity to the current situation so the analogy won't be completely lost on the Performer. This method is effective because it levies no specific criticism and assigns no fault, while allowing the Performer to save face.

**Now go to the Predictive Grid on page 15 and enter a score from 5 to 25 in column B, indicating the degree to which you fit the Performer description.**

## Managing Vulnerability to Performer Superiors

As your boss, a Performer won't remember, much less acknowledge, your achievements or your contributions to departmental work outcomes. He or she also will try mightily to avoid accountability for any negative outcomes by blaming you. To manage this vulnerability, you'll need to document every instruction and keep a record of your achievements. For example, when the Performer boss gives you an assignment, send a quick memo that simply acknowledges that on X date you were asked to do Y task. Once you've completed the task, send another quick memo that informs the boss that Y task was completed on Z date as requested. Have this documentation available at performance review time. Do this openly and conspicuously so that it's apparent that this is your normal business procedure. This way your Performer boss doesn't think he or she is a target. If you've been reporting to a Performer for some time and this would be an obviously new business practice on your part, simply expand the documentation to cover your boss's achievements, too. The document will alleviate the need for your

Performer boss to do the work necessary to feature the accomplishments of those he or she manages.

## Adapting Techniques for Interacting With Performer Superiors

- **Provide extensive administrative support.** Be vigilant about the need to reduce the likelihood of missed details and deadlines.

- **Compliment your Performer boss regularly;** express admiration and support. Although this may seem backward to you, the Performer superior needs your affirmation.

- **Enhance their image.** Rather than making a direct appeal to your Performer boss for whatever it is you want, be indirect, subtly clarifying how doing something will enhance his or her image. "An opportunity for our department might be for me to…." "Something that would differentiate our department from others might be for us to…."

- **Provide reminders** to the Performer boss on everything—more than once.

- **Don't take as gospel what your Performer boss promises.** Realize that a Performer will assure you of various rewards and then claim that someone else prevented his or her following through.

- **Don't engage in business conversation** with the Performer unless you have a way to take notes in real time. Realize that Performers are selective and sporadic listeners. You'll need to protect yourself from the probability of future denials that the conversation, or parts of it, ever took place.

- **Don't rely on the Performer to document your contributions;** document your own achievements.

- **Be friendly. Don't alienate Performers.** It won't help you, and it could hurt you.

- **Be willing to listen to them talk** through their ideas. Ask questions that allow them to pontificate.

## Managing Vulnerability to Performer Subordinates

It's standard operating procedure for Performer subordinates to distort the truth to protect their own images. They think nothing of creating a tapestry of lies and deceit to make themselves look good. If you take action on something a

Performer subordinate tells you without first verifying the story, you're likely to have egg on your face. To manage this vulnerability, check the facts before you act. To reduce the frequency and severity of this vulnerability, link incentives and other forms of recognition to improved teamwork.

## Adapting Techniques for Interacting With Performer Subordinates

- **Be alert to Performers' tendency to miss details** and deadlines. You won't be able to rely on them to read the fine print or to look out for you, so you'll need to develop your own monitoring systems to cover yourself. Indeed, monitor anything that involves or relies on the Performer.

- **Praise them, both publicly and privately.** Performers need praise, so don't withhold it! Realize that praise given by you in private is nice, but insufficient. Compliment them in front of key constituents; include their comments in newsletters or other communiqués; give them recognition.

- **Clarify the career path for your Performer** subordinates. They must always have a carrot in front of them.

- **Clarify the "What's in it for me?" proposition.** Whatever it is that you want from Performer subordinates, you must show how what you want is going to produce gain for them.

- **Verify facts** before believing or acting on what the Performer tells you.

- **Be their audience.** Your Performer subordinate needs to talk and needs you to be an interested listener. Listen with rapt attention whenever possible.

- **Be a cheerleader.** The absence of criticism isn't enough for Performer subordinates. They are easily deflated, so you'll need to actively and frequently encourage them.

- **Help them move from concept to implementation** by getting them to identify specific next steps.

- **Help them showcase their ideas.** Engineer opportunities for Performers to make presentations. Be sure to rehearse with them, since they won't hesitate to provide an extemporaneous delivery.

## Other Styles Performers Find Most Challenging:

- Commanders, for their inescapable "puffery detector" and the imposition of measurable expectations
- Attackers, since they delight in publicly embarrassing others

- Analyticals, because their merciless analysis can expose the Performer's claims as being unsubstantiated

## Typical 360-Degree Input on Performers

Performers want to be valued and validated as being the best. Their unquenchable need for affirmation and favored status forms the basis for most of the following 360-degree input.

### Here's what their superiors have to say:

- *Extremely high maintenance. Is extremely moody. Requires lots of stroking and pouts when it's not forthcoming.*

- *Thinks of himself as real prima donna. Won't rock the boat for the good of the team if doing so will interfere with the image he wants to maintain.*

- *Flaunts pride of accomplishment, ruining effective workplace relationships. Hoards credit.*

- *Thrives on drama and goes out of her way to create it. Sacrifices the trust of the team by acting this way.*

- *Willing to circumvent any rule, covertly if necessary, to achieve status or recognition. Puts personal goals above those of the organization.*

- *Huge ego not proportional to demonstrated accomplishments. Dedicated to building his own empire.*

### Here's what their peers have to say:

- *Poses as a team player but is self-serving. Has elevated the wink to an art form.*

- *Exaggerates the seriousness and urgency of everything to get attention but heads for the tall grass when the pressure is on.*

- *Has a real gift for getting out of work and shoving it onto others.*

- *Abdicates responsibility for failures, yet tries to retain credit for wins.*

- *His need to outshine everyone is so obvious; we joke about him. He's such an attention hog. Even when people are flattering him insincerely, he just laps it up and waits for more.*

- *Very poor listener. Constantly interrupts others to become center of attention. Seems to be suffering when someone else is telling a story with less panache than she would have used.*

## Here's what their subordinates have to say:

- *Needs constant prodding to deliver on commitments. She puts all real work off to the very last minute and then everyone has to rush to cover for her.*

- *Is perpetually and seriously overwhelmed—by his own choice. Takes on projects to gain visibility and recognition and flirts with implosion. Then he overdelegates, shedding the low profile stuff, disengaging from all but the pursuit of high-visibility activities.*

- *Traps us in endless, unproductive conversations from which we cannot extricate ourselves. He just seems to need to be heard pontificating. We have to put in lots of "listening duty" to feed his ego.*

- *Rambles. Is incapable of being concise. Uses abstractness in an effort to establish superiority.*

- *Is frantic and frazzled when, due to own poor self management, everything becomes urgent. We have to pay the price.*

- *Has such a puffed up view of self; uses administrative support as a personal concierge.*

CHAPTER **7**

# The Avoider

DESCRIPTORS

QUIET, RESERVED
STRIVES FOR FLAWLESS PERFORMANCE
FEAR OF RISK
WORRIER
POOR EYE CONTACT
METICULOUS
SPEAKS IN PLATITUDES

RESENTS AND RESISTS CHANGE
LIKES PERSONAL APPROACH
CAUTIOUS, FEARFUL
WON'T GIVE FEEDBACK
NO INITIATIVE
WON'T CONFRONT
WON'T EXPRESS OPINIONS

*L*AUREN, AN AVOIDER CFO, WAS MARGINALIZED, *overlooked, and disenfranchised by her CEO. Multiple rescheduling was required for every meeting she set with him because he perpetually "blew her off." He delayed any review of financial operations, rushed through complicated financial models of crucial importance to the health of the organization, and trivialized her concerns about his wildly fluctuating compensation and bonus practices. Although she was deeply offended and hurt by this treatment and was encouraged by numerous colleagues and associates to discuss it with him, she chose never to confront the CEO.*

Mild mannered, professorial, and soft spoken, Avoiders are the wallflowers of the world. They keep a low profile, don't seek the limelight, and don't make waves. Lauren, for example, would never dream of confronting her boss as her colleagues advised. More important to Avoiders is the absence of discord. They create warm, cozy, nestlike environments that are softly lit with lamps rather than overhead lighting. In this inviting setting, they exude an aura of wisdom and approachability that makes it easy for others to confide in them. Highly perceptive, gently inquisitive, and attentive listeners, Avoiders will be both engaged and engaging as long as they are not the topic of conversation. Extremely slow to establish personal relationships, Avoiders prefer to keep interactions light and casual.

Their responses to personal questions are uttered with what appears to be carefully considered self-reflection but is actually poor eye contact caused by the urgent need to shift the topic toward superficial small talk. This creates just enough mystery to make them simultaneously alluring and slightly disconcerting. In fact, what masquerades as mystery and wisdom actually conceals a fear of being "found out." Their discomfort with any substantive conversation about themselves is grounded in the belief that once you know who they are or what they think, your opinion of them, your esteem for them, will be eroded.

When interacting with others, Avoiders participate comfortably in social chitchat but won't express their opinions or discuss issues that may require them to take a stand. If asked directly for an opinion, they'll dodge the question by eloquently summarizing the various possible viewpoints, acknowledging the complexities, but taking no position. They use open ended questions as a deflecting tactic.

When required to work on a team or committee, they speak only to validate what others have said or to seek clarity about another's opinion. Even if an Avoider has a great idea, he or she won't share it for fear that others will think it stupid or wrong. If someone else offers the same idea and is criticized, the Avoider is secretly relieved; if the idea is validated, the Avoider is secretly angry.

*In multiple coaching sessions, marketing manager Kira and her boss developed action plans to address her various problems with collegial interactions. Week after week, they discussed permutations of the same issues, and developed permutations of the same action plans, yet Kira never took any positive steps. What she ultimately had to acknowledge was that she found it infinitely preferable to bemoan her current state than to adopt a solution orientation, make a commitment to improving the situation, and take an action that would advance the ball.*

Although they may indeed be discontent, Avoiders like Kira complain to uninvolved others rather than engage with relevant parties to solve problems. They'll complain about work while at home; they'll complain about home while at work; but they wouldn't dream of paving the way for retaliatory criticism by taking their complaints to the appropriate parties. If present during the conflicts of others, they're incredibly adroit at flat-lining their emotions and adopting the role of counselor. They don't advise; they synthesize. They don't make suggestions, but they elicit and reframe suggestions made by those involved.

*Larry, the equipment and facilities manager, acknowledged that one of his employees was openly defiant, divisive, and disrespectful but refused to discipline him for fear that*

*(a) things would just get worse; (b) a competent replacement couldn't be found; (c) the employee would use his connections to gain sympathy from key stakeholders. Even when complainants threatened to go over Larry's head, he took no action.*

Avoiders' reticence to deal with unpleasant truths manifests itself in the performance review process, where Avoiders obscure critical feedback in platitudes and clichés that leave you frustrated and confused. When it comes to confronting poor performance, as in this example, what looks like patience on Larry's part is actually an unwillingness to confront. The same is true regarding introspection. Already disappointed with their conscious self-knowledge, they're loath to uncover even more about which to be disappointed.

As delegates, Avoiders take copious notes that capture all content, including innuendo, but they commit you to absolutely nothing. They provide comprehensive briefings with fluency and confidence, analyzing all the options, but they don't make recommendations without including the indemnifying preface: "If you want X, then I recommend…."

Avoiders tend toward solitary work. Appealing to them is the obscurity of being a cog in a large bureaucracy, the safety of being in a highly regulated profession such as finance, or the insulation of being a "super geek" in a field such as science or technology. Common to these choices is the likelihood of minimal scrutiny. In a bureaucracy, one can easily become anonymous; in highly regulated fields, there are absolutes; and in the stratosphere of "geekdom," no one understands enough about what's going on to be able to impose scrutiny.

Policies and procedures manuals are absolutely essential to Avoiders. By providing the comfort and protection of rules and precedent, these manuals negate any requirement for Avoiders to use their judgment, which meets their need to be blameless. Cloaked in documented process, Avoiders can safely adhere without being exposed to ridicule. Without the guidelines of tradition, precedent, or rules, Avoiders are paralyzed. They will choose to do nothing rather than incur the risk attendant to taking initiative. That this trait can prevent them from obtaining greater responsibilities is not an unwelcome consequence. Increased responsibility imposes undesirable levels of visibility and accountability, both of which the Avoider scrupulously shuns. They will sacrifice money, position, growth, and new opportunities for the safety of status quo and will suffer the lack of job satisfaction for the assurance of a job for life or for an expanded retirement plan. Their organizational loyalty emanates not from a sense of fidelity but from fear of change and fear of risk.

*28-year-old Lionel, a coordinator in IT, sat across the breakfast table from his coach and complained wearily that he had lost respect for his boss, didn't enjoy the nature of his work, was uncomfortable around the people with whom he worked, and wasn't emotionally wedded to the mission of the organization for which he was working. Because his technology skills were very much in demand, the coach inquired why he would remain in such a position when he could easily get the job of his choosing. Lionel immediately replied, "Because of retirement!" "Do you mean to tell me," the coach asked, "that you would stay in a job you hate, working for someone you disesteem, with people you don't enjoy, for a cause you don't endorse, just to ensure your retirement, when you're only 28?" Without hesitation, and with a look of real surprise, Lionel said, "Of course!"*

So what is it that makes Avoiders avoid? Fear. Fear about what? Pretty much everything. From the moment their feet touch the floor upon waking until they fall asleep, Avoiders are preoccupied with negative fantasies about the punitive consequences that might accrue from anything they do. As a result, Avoiders are risk averse and change averse in the extreme. Change can be immobilizing for Avoiders because it increases their vulnerability to mistakes. Making mistakes causes feelings of incompetence, exacerbating their already low self-confidence. As Lionel's story so clearly depicts, for Avoiders, the devil they know is better than the devil they don't.

Although it's their omnipresent fear of negative consequences that makes their own work outputs reliably error free, Avoiders aren't fear-laden about the mistakes of others. Instead, they react calmly and reassuringly when others make mistakes. They don't impose recriminations on others, primarily because they don't want to suffer recriminations themselves. Any type of criticism makes Avoiders feel threatened. Even a mild reproach convinces them that termination is imminent. As a result, Avoiders are extremely meticulous about their work. When receiving assignments, they'll do precisely what they are told and not a smidgen less—but not a smidgen more either.

Avoiders look at Commanders and wish they had the confidence to lead others; they look at Drifters and wish they were willing to share fledgling ideas; they look at Attackers and wish they had the guts to confront others; they look at Pleasers and wish they had the courage to wear their hearts on their sleeves; they look at Performers and wish they had the courage to be center stage; and they look at Analyticals and wish they had the temerity to question others. Avoiders trivialize their own numerous and significant strengths and see themselves as less adequate than all others. Well-intentioned suggestions that they use their considerable skills and talents to move up the ladder can backfire. Avoiders are predisposed to construe your suggestions as evidence that you consider who they are right now to be inadequate. Because they already see themselves this way, any indication, even if only implied, that your thoughts align with this view is especially painful to them.

Contradictory though it may seem, this particular situation can evoke outbursts from the Avoider that display the most hostile of Attacker traits. Although short-lived and usually followed by long periods of silence, such fury from Avoiders is no less intense than had it emanated from an Attacker. Feelings of blame can also catalyze this reactionary metamorphosis. Even when legitimately faulted, the Avoider's hypersensitivity to an inadequate self-view can spark a scathing tantrum.

*Since Jack's wife initiated divorce proceedings, he has been drinking excessively at association events, embarrassing himself and others. Louise, Jack's secretary, has repeatedly appealed to Jack's best friend Joe, asking him to have a talk with Jack, but Joe has remained silent because he doesn't want to create additional trouble for Jack at this painful time in his life. Louise has also approached their CEO, Sherene, expressing concern about Jack's safety and the impact of his drinking. Sherene refuses to take punitive action because she sees the situation as potentially litigious and doesn't want to be party to a law suit. Jack ultimately dies in a car accident while driving home after an event. Joe is mad at Sherene because he thinks she should have used her position to confront Jack. Sherene is mad at Joe because she thinks Joe should have used his friendship to confront Jack. Louise is furious with both of them, since neither took action.*

All but Louise in this story were Avoiders—Jack because he was trying to avoid his own issues, Joe because he wouldn't confront his friend, Sherene because she wouldn't confront the problem. The point is that Avoiders don't take action when taking action is appropriate and rationalize away any responsibility for the ensuing results.

## Greatest Strengths

Avoiders are highly motivated to produce flawless work. Whatever the task, they go to great lengths to ensure it's done right the first time, every time, with meticulous attention to detail. Reliable, predictable, and content with a low profile, Avoiders are low-maintenance employees who don't make waves.

## Greatest Need

More than anything, Avoiders want security. The elusive nature of this need can incapacitate Avoiders. Because they define security as the absence of risk and see risk in every initiative, decision, change, or opinion, they're in a constant state of fear and unrest. Every behavior, every decision, every day, is formatted by them to minimize risk.

## Decision Method

The only decision method that the Avoider finds sufficiently insulating is group decision making. Avoiders are more comfortable with "we" than with "me" and will delay decision making until they can convene the protection of appropriate additional parties or receive an explicit directive from above. Even if it dwarfs their careers, the safety and security of diminished individual responsibility is essential to Avoiders.

## Reaction to Feedback

When receiving critical feedback, Avoiders hear only the first few words. After that, their systems shut down. They see your lips moving, but they can't take in what you're saying. Their faces reveal nothing about how they're feeling, and they say nothing. You can't even tell if you're getting through. When they think you're finished, they'll ask to be excused and slip quietly out the door. Although it may not appear to be so, they are absolutely terrified. Convinced that they're on extremely thin ice, they're overwhelmed with fear. The next time you ask for a meeting, they'll expect to be terminated. To prevent the Avoider's discomfiture, precede your critique with references to a future that includes the Avoider: "Next year we're going to…"; "Five years from now, when we…." Follow this with "but for now we need to…" or "At the moment, though, I need your help to…."

**Now go to the Predictive Grid on page 15 and enter a score from 5 to 25 in column B, Indicating the degree to which you fit the Avoider description.**

## Managing Vulnerability to the Avoider Superior

As your boss, the Avoider makes you vulnerable by not taking on any new or high-profile projects through which you could distinguish yourself. Avoiders are not ambitious on their own behalf or yours and don't provide opportunities for you to move up. There are three steps to neutralizing this dilemma.

- **Identify a project or a team you'd like to work on.** Determine whether, contingent upon your boss's approval, you'd be a welcome addition.

- **Next, determine specifically how you can add this new activity** to your workload without the potential for erosion in the quality or the quantity of what you're already doing for the Avoider boss. If this new activity will reduce your hours of work for the Avoider, explain how you'll ensure the work will still get done.

- **Finally, eliminate the risk that any accountability would accrue** to your Avoider boss in the event you fail in your new endeavor. Suggest a dotted line to whomever your additional tasks would make you responsible, so that your performance in that arena is discrete from your performance for the Avoider. Present the risk-free plan to your Avoider boss. They're usually willing to accommodate your desire to reach for the brass ring, as long as doing so doesn't put them at risk.

## Adapting Techniques for Interacting With Avoider Superiors

- **Keep your Avoider boss informed** about whatever you know. Minimize surprises.

- **Come alongside your Avoider boss** early in the change process and work to increase the time period he or she has to adjust. For example, if new technology is being brought in, provide (or ensure the appropriate person provides) individual training sessions.

- **Provide assistance in evaluating risk.** When you know your Avoider boss is facing a tough decision, think through the options and the implications in advance and either provide these in writing or initiate discussions with your boss about the options.

- **If you plan to be out, talk about it** as far in advance as you possibly can, being specific about how your work will be handled in your absence.

- **Don't speak loudly or become emotional** in the presence of your Avoider boss, even if these behaviors are directed at someone else. If the Avoider is present, it's important to maintain low-key behavior.

- **Don't intrude into the personal life** of the Avoider. Be friendly, but keep it about business.

- **Slow down when communicating** with your Avoider boss. It's not that you have to be particularly slow, just don't be hyper in speech or in movement.

- **Don't demonstrate your career aspirations** in ways that threaten or surprise the Avoider. Be sure your Avoider boss is the first to know about your plans and isn't caught off guard or embarrassed by others' advance knowledge.

- **Be candid and open** with the Avoider; don't earn his or her suspicion.

## Managing Vulnerability to the Avoider Subordinate

The complete absence of any initiative on the part of the Avoider can be so frustrating as to cause you to lose your temper. If you tell Avoider subordinates to do steps 1, 2, and 3, and it's obvious that step 4 comes next, realize that Avoiders won't do 4, because they're convinced you had a reason for not telling them to do it. Losing your patience with initiative-averse Avoiders is disabling and unproductive for them. Instead, accept that you'll always need to provide detailed instructions to Avoiders, and acknowledge them for their as-requested completion of the work.

## Adapting Techniques for Interacting With Avoider Subordinates

- **Insulate and protect them.** Clarify how doing whatever it is you want Avoiders to do will shield them from unwanted risk, attention, and responsibility.

- **Don't thrust sudden change on the Avoider.** Talk about it in advance and in detail, providing time for the Avoider to adjust. Be sure to discuss implications for the Avoider's daily worklife or routine.

- **Maintain as stable a work environment as possible.** Don't initiate change just for the sake of change or to sate your own need for newness.

- **Act quickly to calm the Avoider** when change is imminent by emphasizing the similarities between the old and the new and by providing a clear and detailed transition plan.

- **Don't talk to the Avoider when you're angry.**

- **Don't put Avoiders in situations** that require high initiative or judgment calls.

- **Don't rush through meetings or discussions.** Slow down. Allow time for them to ask questions.

- **Don't threaten the Avoider.** Doing so serves no constructive purpose and renders the Avoider unable to perform. Instead, discuss what specific next steps are required.

- **Reaffirm their positive traits.** Avoiders feel competent and confident only for moments at a time, and those moments are fleeting. Accept that there's no such thing as enough affirmation for Avoiders.

- **Provide ongoing reassurances of job security.** Frequently confirm the utility of their job functions and the perpetual need for their services.

- **Don't try to cajole or bully the Avoider** into taking on more responsibility.

## Other Styles Avoiders Find Most Challenging
- Commanders, whose initiative and action orientation terrify Avoiders
- Attackers, whose unpredictable scathing tirades keep Avoiders in a constant state of anxiety
- Performers, for their attention seeking, opportunistic natures

## Actual 360-Degree Input on Avoiders
Avoiders want to be valued and validated for their behind-the-scenes contributions and for the sanctuary they provide to those weary of expectations and accountabilities. But as this 360-degree input makes clear, the inaction orientation exhibited by Avoiders generates considerable frustration.

### Here's what their superiors have to say:
- *Waits to be invited to demonstrate value, rather than stepping up to do so. Clearly has no desire for expanded responsibilities.*

- *It's painfully obvious how reserved and guarded this individual is. Very self-protective, debilitated by criticism.*

- *Over-reliance on rules, is paralyzed and incapacitated in the absence of direction.*

- *Delivers what is asked, but never raises the bar or sets stretch goals. Absolutely cannot multitask.*

- *Clutches in high-pressure situations. Cannot think on her feet or adapt on the fly.*

- *Style is so low key as to seem ineffective; erodes faith in leadership.*

## Here's what their peers have to say:

- *Too timid and introverted to be an effective leader or advocate, is passive and submissive. Gives up and backs off at the first sign of resistance.*

- *So collaborative as to be unable to make decisions.*

- *Won't say or do anything controversial or provocative. Should be willing to express opinions more readily, to champion challenges, and ruffle feathers when necessary.*

- *Apparent lack of confidence erodes whatever competence may exist.*

- *Nonjudgmental. This has real costs, and they outweigh the benefits when such a person is in a management or leadership position.*

- *Uses waiting as a strategy. Holds back and waits for others to take the lead.*

## Here's what their subordinates have to say:

- *Ignores internal friction within and between departments even when it hinders performance.*

- *Does not exude or inspire confidence.*

- *My boss acknowledges that the volume of work is crushing and cannot be sustained, yet will not take appropriate next steps. His defeatist attitude, which he thinks is just realism, prevents him from submitting justifications for additional staff or establishing criteria for accepting new work.*

- *The same problems keep recurring because my boss won't even acknowledge that there is a problem.*

- *Uses email as a way to sidestep unpleasantness or confrontation.*

- *Won't go to the wall on important issues. Doesn't stick up for staff, even if he agrees that staff is being treated unfairly.*

# CHAPTER 8

# The Analytical

DESCRIPTORS

| | |
|---|---|
| PRECISE, DILIGENT | DATA ORIENTED |
| NOT INNOVATIVE | DETAILED |
| CAUTIOUS | PROCRASTINATES |
| TUNNEL VISION | OVERANALYZES EVERYTHING |
| MONOTONE | WORRIES ABOUT "WHAT IF" |
| AVOIDS CLOSURE | POOR EYE CONTACT |
| CHECKS EVERYTHING THRICE | FOCUSES ON PROCESS |
| NOT SPONTANEOUS | MANAGES BY MEMO |

*T*HEO, AN *ANALYTICAL* CEO, CONSTANTLY CHANGED *the variables used in business calculations for measuring organizational performance and iteratively reformatted board documents weeks, days, and even hours before board meetings. Compounding the already arduous preparations for these meetings, his endless quest for perfection generated untold days of rework and much more stress than was necessary to get the job done, changing well rehearsed presentations of others moments before their delivery. Modifications varied with each meeting, were impossible to anticipate, and always resulted in extensive changes to numerous collateral materials. Significant tweaking continued up to the last minute. Pleas for mercy from his senior staff went unheeded, since Theo saw his changes as qualitative improvements that he had a fiduciary responsibility to deliver.*

Deliberate, precise, and logical, Analyticals like Theo can be the personification of bottlenecks. Their almost compulsive need to check and recheck, to verify and reverify, can provoke others to the point that they band together in a veritable underground movement dedicated to circumventing the Analytical. Their slow-as-molasses, iterative, process-laden approach hijacks projects and impedes productivity to the extent that their colleagues blatantly taunt any consequence rather than adhere to requirements for interaction with Analyticals.

Decide what level of engagement you're seeking from the Analytical. If you merely want to inform, say so, or write on the document, "for information only; no action required." If you want the Analytical to participate in a single meeting or event with no further action required, say so, or write on the document, "this event only; no further action being requested." If you don't specify either of these levels of engagement, Analyticals will adopt their default position, which is fully involved, assuming you want them to handle the whole project. Misunderstandings about the level of engagement can cause redundancies and rework, so clarify the Analytical's involvement up front.

Succinct and accurate are mutually exclusive terms in the mind of the Analytical. As a result, they have a tough time with brevity. This is what drives them to deliver prolonged, comprehensive presentations. If they have to choose between the legibility of their PowerPoint slides and providing what they believe is essential information, they'll reduce font size to 10 and margins to zero so that every single number can appear on the screen.

*In senior staff meetings, if anyone asked Cullen, the chief technology officer, a question, all others present would roll their eyes, look down at the table, and cringe. After the meeting, the questioner would hastily be taken aside and made to feel like a mutineer for committing the unpardonable sin of "activating Cullen," exposing all present to his interminable verbosity.*

There's just no such thing as a short answer from an Analytical. Recognizing the numerous variables embedded within any question, Analyticals like Cullen are precise in the extreme and feel compelled, literally duty-bound, to accommodate all permutations of the question with multiple answers. Similarly, they feel a fiduciary responsibility to thoroughly vet any new idea by anticipating all possible outcomes of implementation, assigning probabilities to each possible outcome, and identifying the likely radial impacts of each possible outcome. By the time they've completed their evaluations, they've choked the life out of the idea and suffocated any enthusiasm others may have had for it.

But smothering innovation isn't Analyticals' intent. Instead, their objective is to expose risk, thereby enabling neutralization of risk, resulting in enhanced success. It is their failure to edit apparent negativity out of their analyses that results in Analyticals being likened to storm clouds that rain on others' parades.

Resentful of accusations that they disesteem the bottom line, Analyticals see themselves as its protectors and won't be rushed. Using hype and emotionalism to try to expedite the Analytical's process only evokes suspicions of recklessness, puts them on high alert, and slows them down.

*Volumes of correspondence and formal comments are processed in Wilma's department daily. Veteran staff draft appropriate responses for her signature as senior director. Without exception, Wilma alters these work products in ways that don't enhance the result. Primarily, her changes are stylistic rather than substantive. In addition to redlining the document, Wilma requires face-to-face meetings that are completely redundant to the red-lining, consuming otherwise allocated time slots. She then complains when overtime increases or completed work doesn't permit enough time for her extensive review.*

Immune to expressions of exasperation with their methods, Analyticals like Wilma become indignant when asked to short-cut or side-step their standard operating procedures. More important than what is being done is how it's being done, so irrespective of their commitment to goal achievement, the Analytical's contribution as a leader will be to method, not to vision.

Contemplative by nature, they just can't think "light" and are painfully aware of their ineptitude with the frivolity and gaiety of social events. Stiff and formal, Analyticals can be immobilized when expected to be extemporaneous. Asking them to say a few words with no chance to prepare can incapacitate them to the point that they stumble over their words, their unease apparent to everyone.

Because instant replay functionality can't be applied to workplace interactions, Analyticals prefer to manage by memo. Prioritizing documentation over conversation insulates their analyses from the unpredictability of human behavior and provides an archive of irrefutable evidence that can be read and reread. This reticence to engage verbally extends to physical contact. Beyond a handshake, they don't want to be touched.

Although it's invisible to observers, Analyticals are perpetually engaged in cognitive multitasking. Tantamount to solving multiple, simultaneous equations, this impressive ability has the disadvantage of rendering the Analytical monotone and causing poor eye contact. Coupled with their social awkwardness, this quality unfairly casts Analyticals as being dull and boring. Indeed, given the choice of attending a social event or moving boxes at the annual meeting site, Analyticals would prefer the backache.

## Greatest Strengths

Analyticals can see 10 steps farther out than everyone else. Not only can they forecast with uncanny accuracy, but they can also calculate the probabilities of various business scenarios and predict the radial impacts of each. They are highly skilled at evaluating risks far enough in advance to enable mitigation and are fluent with both deductive and inductive reasoning. Their commitment to accuracy and their keen sense of organizational stewardship combine to position them as trustworthy colleagues.

## Greatest Need

In everything they do, Analyticals have a consuming need to be absolutely, positively correct. Before taking any action, before choosing a course, before making a recommendation or a decision, Analyticals need unassailable certainty. Since, as the saying goes, nothing is certain but death and taxes, Analyticals are in a perpetual state of discomfort.

## Decision Method

Analyticals have great difficulty coming to closure about anything. Their insistence on certainty makes them notorious procrastinators. Always preferring to delay their decisions in favor of obtaining more data, Analyticals will analyze and reanalyze in an endless struggle to eliminate ambiguity. Ultimately, they either surrender the decision-making responsibility to someone else and accept an advisory role, or they make decisions only when delay is no longer possible and they're forced to do so.

## Reaction to Feedback

Analyticals are open to critical feedback only if you have examples to back it up. The absence of specific examples invalidates your feedback and absolves the Analytical of any responsibility to take it seriously. Additionally, Analyticals have what they believe to be a good reason or a logical explanation for absolutely everything they say and do. Before they acknowledge any flaw or misstep, expect to hear a detailed justification of their actions.

**Now go to the Predictive Grid on page 15 and enter a score from 5 to 25 in column B, indicating the degree to which you fit the Analytical description.**

## Managing Vulnerability to Analytical Superiors

As bosses, Analyticals make you vulnerable by never letting you out from under the microscope. Mistakes are unthinkable, and if you make one, it'll be years before the Analytical boss trusts you again. To gain increased independence, you'll need to ensure that the work you submit is consistently, reliably error free. Proof your work to the last decimal point, more than once. With more complex or lengthy assignments, ask someone else to also proof your work. It's much easier to avoid mistakes in the first place than to have to earn your way out from under the Analytical's distrust.

## Adapting Techniques for Interacting With Analytical Superiors

- **Summarize discussions** with your Analytical boss in writing.

- **Pay attention to how Analyticals structure their documents.** Adopt their format. They'll be more receptive if the appearance of your work reflects their standard approach to issues.

- **Communicate, summarize, condense, and analyze** with matrices, charts, or graphs.

- **Ask Analyticals what data, methods, or processes** they'd like you to use when doing your work. Establishing this in advance helps avoid rework.

- **Present step-by-step reasoning** when attempting to persuade the Analytical. Show specifically how each fact builds on the next and how these facts lead to certain conclusions that suggest specific actions.

- **Always be prepared to answer lots of questions** without becoming exasperated.

- **Speak their language.** Become fluent with data, important ratios, and relevant metrics.

- **Benchmark. Compare and contrast.** Don't make seat-of-the-pants recommendations. Cite sources; demonstrate that you've done your research.

- **Don't withhold technical information** just because it's out of the Analytical's realm of expertise. Analyticals will do their homework and become competent very quickly.

- **Don't rush Analyticals** and don't create unnecessary urgencies. Remember, they become suspicious and slow down when you rush them.

- **Don't expect instantaneous decisions** from your Analytical boss. When Analyticals say they need time to think it over, they mean it!

- **Check your work** at least twice.

- **Don't create unnecessary urgencies.** Your oversights discomfit the Analytical. Plan and schedule your work, adhering conspicuously to both.

- **Be explicit with your questions.** If you don't parameterize your inquiries, the Analytical's answers will consider all permutations and will be unnecessarily voluminous.

## Managing Vulnerability to Analytical Subordinates

Analytical subordinates make you vulnerable by not meeting deadlines or by requesting extensions at the last moment. Their motto is, "Do you want it now, or do you want it right? You can't have both!" To manage your vulnerability to the deadline-phobic Analytical subordinate, you'll need to randomly vary the use of two different tactics:

- When an Analytical subordinate asks you to extend a deadline, you can insist that the deadline be met but offer immunity if your insistence on now ultimately reveals that waiting would have been wiser.

- Assign firm start and end dates for a project, and then require Analytical subordinates to break down the project into multiple components, assigning their own interim deadlines to each. Monitor the deadlines to ensure that progress remains on track.

## Adapting Techniques for Interacting With Analytical Subordinates

- **Don't demean data.** As part of their job requirements, Analyticals are often tasked with producing detailed reports and are offended if others recoil when expected to read them. Instead of wincing at the sight of their voluminous tome, accept it with thanks and establish a date to review it together. In the interim, highlight a few sentences to inquire about later. During the meeting, when an Analytical realizes that you took the trouble to at least scan his or her report, any previous transgressions will be instantly forgiven, and you'll enjoy enhanced cooperation from the Analytical.

- **Express appreciation for being able to rely on Analyticals** for accurate data and for their fluency with that data.

- **Provide instructions in writing** whenever possible. Use tracking functions and be prepared to explain your edits.

- **Don't expect extemporaneous input** from Analytical subordinates.

- **Help Analytical subordinates learn how to construct executive summaries.**

- **Monitor the deadlines** for which your Analytical subordinate is responsible.

- **Consider carefully** whether it's really necessary to deploy an Analytical subordinate as a team member.

- **Set precise limits on rework.** Help Analytical subordinates recognize when enough is enough regarding quantity of data and analysis.

- **Don't ask Analyticals to immediately express opinions** or make instantaneous recommendations. Give them time to consider.

- **Help them achieve a neutral tone.** Coach your Analytical subordinate to pose questions in a way that doesn't indicate pessimism.

## Other Styles Analyticals Find Most Challenging:
- Commanders, for their willingness to act in the absence of, even in defiance of, data
- Drifters, for their inattention to detail and deadlines
- Performers, for their image-driven misrepresentations

## Actual 360-Degree Input on Analyticals
Analyticals want to be valued and validated for their accuracy and for their ability to assess risk. Although their strengths are undeniably necessary, even crucial, this 360-degree input makes clear that the time and tedium required to interact with the Analytical can be a source of extreme exasperation for colleagues.

## Here's what their superiors have to say:
- *We lose opportunities, staff, and even revenue because of her inability to make decisions.*
- *Often overprepares self and staff, reaching the point of diminishing returns.*
- *Unable to accept decisions contrary to own view.*
- *Great manager of process—lousy manager of people.*
- *Takes no change in stride.*

- *Her unyielding insistence that business be conducted in an unattainably risk-free environment impedes rather than enables the business of our association.*

## Here's what their peers have to say:

- *Drowns self and others in mundane details. We don't interact with him anymore because we just don't have the time or the patience for his minutiae orientation.*

- *We work around this individual. We have to. Otherwise, every idea for improvement would be shot down and strangled.*

- *Her rigidity, her need for absolute perfection, holds individuals and the organization back; makes us weaker, not stronger.*

- *Impedes others who advocate change, even when those changes would fix things that are broken.*

- *Once she has come to a conclusion about something, it is impossible to persuade her to make adjustments, even if circumstances warrant it.*

- *People have always been a distant second to data. Is detached and without compassion.*

## Here's what their subordinates have to say:

- *We are always watched, questioned, and checked. Every move we make throughout the day is scrutinized. He makes us acutely aware that we are not trusted.*

- *We have to nag and nag and nag for decisions from her. Then we get one line email responses that don't advance the ball. Decisions have to be wrenched from her. It's just anguish.*

- *Our internal departmental reputation has been ruined because her endless, minor changes delay everything. She creates a huge bottleneck.*

- *We're expected to maintain instantaneous fluency with massive amounts of data. We are asked questions in public venues on an impromptu basis about complicated data and are made to feel her disappointment if we cannot answer immediately.*

- *Every single step of a project has to be continually reviewed, rejustified, and reapproved. Even rework gets reworked. Nothing is ever final.*

- *Utterly without humanness; merciless, never-ending doggedness. Almost machine-like. Works every weekend even when there's no crisis and expects us to do the same. Views those who have a different work ethic as slackers.*

# CHAPTER 9

# Your Achiever as The Chameleon's Edge

### DESCRIPTORS

CONFIDENT

INSPIRATIONAL

HIGH SELF-ESTEEM

PEACEFUL

CONTENT

HONORABLE

INTERESTED IN OTHERS' OPINIONS

AUTHENTIC

VALUE-BASED BEHAVIOR

PERCEPTIVE

CONSTRUCTIVE

COMMITMENT ORIENTED

PERSONABLE

KNOWLEDGEABLE

EFFECTIVE

NO HIDDEN AGENDA

WISE

GENEROUS

WHICHEVER OF THE SEVEN behavioral styles seems most like you, the above adjectives are also descriptive of you—when you're at your best. Unlike the seven behavioral styles already presented, the Achiever is not a separate style. Instead, the Achiever permeates all the styles to varying degrees, depending on your level of awareness and self-discipline. When the Achiever dominates your behavior, your strengths are augmented and your rough edges are muted. The Achiever coexists with your template of styles and influences the degree to which you exhibit the best or the worst of those styles. You'll learn more about the impact your Achiever score can have on your behavior, including how to increase your Achiever score, in Chapter 10. For now, here's a quick look at how each of the seven behavioral styles is affected when the Achiever dominates:

- A pure Commander needs to control everything and everyone. The Achiever-Commander recognizes the importance of letting others lead and doesn't seek to dominate every situation.

- A pure Drifter isn't attentive enough to realize the impact of his or her disorganization. The Achiever-Drifter can be relied upon to comply with structural norms in the workplace.

- A pure Attacker makes no effort to edit the abusive tone out of his or her communications. The Achiever-Attacker is keenly aware of the need to do so and aggressively self-monitors.

- The pure Pleaser endures tremendous personal strain to maintain relationships. The Achiever-Pleaser is willing to confront when necessary.

- The pure Performer has an insatiable need for recognition. The Achiever-Performer realizes the importance of recognition and is diligent to notice others' strengths and compliment their efforts.

- The pure Avoider is risk averse in the extreme. The Achiever-Avoider is willing to act independently, even in the absence of precedent.

- The pure Analytical procrastinates interminably. The Achiever-Analytical is willing to make decisions even when desired information isn't available.

In your Achiever mode, interpersonal versatility equips you to consistently behave in ways that nourish and sustain the dignity of others without sacrificing authenticity. Able to rally disparate others toward collaborative behavior, you respond to the provocative actions of others with great poise and without apparent effort.

When your Achiever is governing your behavior, you're able to reach through others' mistakes; see through their inflammatory, inciting acts; and inspire them to regain their footing. In your presence, others see the best of themselves, as if they're immersed in a reservoir of every good thing they've ever done, every smart move they've made, every selfless act committed, and every personal best achieved. You seem to shine with belief in others, delighting in their achievements and emitting a confidence in them that heartens and strengthens.

Without formality or explicitness, without lecture or conviction, time in your presence steadies, revitalizes, and refreshes others, motivating them to reformat their behavior so that their own Achiever dominates. Your almost imperceptible, perhaps even unconscious, changes in eye contact and posture blend into an indefinable aura that urges from others their best and highest selves. Particularly worthy of note is that others are not ambivalent about disappointing the Achiever side of you. Instead, they step up because the Achiever in you makes them believe they can; they hunker down because you make them want to; they endure because they know that's what you would do. And in the subsequent moments of quiet, priceless acknowledgement from you, they are radiant, hungry for another chance to surpass themselves—in large part as a way to honor you.

Even when you know the answers to others' problems and can clearly see the best path forward, the Achiever in you prevents you from saying, "Here's what you should do next," or "Here's what you should have done." Instead, you allow the answers to emerge from others, to originate in and emanate from them. Without saying much, you create for others the kinds of opportunities that result in affirming self-discovery. You display an awareness of and a regard for their efforts, struggles, and strivings and then find ways to feature their learning.

Introspective and self-assured in your Achiever state, you welcome account- ability and unhesitatingly take responsibility for your outcomes. Genuinely, perpetually interested in learning and improving, you extend a warm and recep- tive welcome to criticism, are quick to acknowledge your own shortcomings, and are able to laugh at your own foibles. Grounded by the seemingly endless emotional endurance of your Achiever, you're gracious about the missteps and rough edges of others and aren't soured by the choices they make. Your keen discernment based on the practiced observation of others equips you to adapt easily, optimizing interactions with anyone, anytime, anywhere.

The more your behavior reflects Achiever descriptors, the more willing others are to tell you the unvarnished truth. Even if the news is bad, the Achiever in you receives the news as information and packages your response appropri- ately, helping you achieve needed results. When your Achiever is in the driver's seat, you're more conscious of your behavior—whatever your dominant style is—and more engaged in active governance of your behavior. As a result, you're more frequently victorious in the battle to subordinate feelings to results. Your disciplined adherence to versatility cloaks you in a state of unflappable serenity, regardless of what's happening around you. This helps nourish your own self- esteem and sustains others' esteem for you. What a powerful example you provide in not allowing your behavior to be dictated by the actions or disposi- tions of others!

## Greatest Strength

Tapping into the Achiever in you allows you to access the strengths of every other behavioral style. This versatility is The Chameleon's Edge—a competitively differentiating characteristic that sets you apart from most others. Your Achiever's versatility enables you to adopt, or adapt immediately to, any of the seven behav- ioral styles with fluency and grace, exhibiting only the best of each. Alert to the

utility of behavior as a tool for securing needed business results, your Achiever helps you make a cognitive choice about which style to deploy with whom and increases your diligence in editing out the rough edges attendant to each.

## Greatest Need

The Achiever's greatest need is for competence. Three important points about this need: First, unlike the other seven behavioral styles whose greatest needs can only be fulfilled by others, competence cannot be attained vicariously or by proxy. Instead, only you can satisfy your Achiever's need for competence. Second, having achieved the desired level of competence, your Achiever is not reliant on others to sustain it. Finally, because your need for competence isn't driven by the need to extract something from others, such as control, freedom, respect, relationships, recognition, security, or certainty, you are less reliant on external assessment. Your Achiever holds you and only you accountable for attaining and maintaining that which you most need. Since your interactions aren't need-driven, you'll be interpersonally effective even in the toughest situations.

## Decision Method

While decision making by each of the seven behavioral styles is linked to their greatest needs (control, freedom, respect, relationships, recognition, security, or certainty), the Achiever in you has no self-serving agenda. When you allow the Achiever to dominate your behavior, you make decisions based on what will be most effective. Because others can sense this, acceptance of your decisions is virtually assured.

## Reaction to Feedback

Achievers consider the opinions of others, are receptive to alternate points of view, and actively seek feedback from others. If you're in an Achiever state when you receive critical feedback, you'll be attentive, inviting elaboration and clarity; you'll acknowledge your role in any conflict, taking ownership for your behavior; and you'll make appropriate adjustments.

**Now go to the Predictive Grid on page 15 and enter a score from 5 to 25 in column B, indicating the degree to which you fit the Achiever description.**

## Managing Vulnerabilities and Adapting Techniques for Achievers

When the Achiever is dominant in your behavior, interacting with you doesn't pose any vulnerability to others and doesn't require any alteration or adaptation by others. Unlike those who resent any suggestion that they adapt to others, the Achiever mindset values the results that ensue from demonstrated versatility and doesn't begrudge the fact that adapting is necessary. Comparatively remarkable about Achiever-dominated styles is that they don't expect others to do the adapting. Those who haven't studied behavioral patterns may not realize what they're witnessing when Achiever versatility is deliberately deployed, but the absence of specific knowledge doesn't diminish their realization that someone special is in their midst. Those who are able to discern your intentional, disciplined striving-toward-Achiever behavior are no less inspired by it.

## How Achievers Accommodate Multiple Styles Simultaneously

Workshop attendees often ask how Achievers can adapt successfully in groups where multiple behavioral styles are present, especially when the message to be delivered is particularly provocative. It is indeed possible to articulate messages for multiple styles; it just takes a little extra time to craft customized messaging so it resonates with multiple others. Here's an example.

Suppose you're asking the board to approve a dues increase and that all seven behavioral styles are on your board. Naturally, you'll want to lobby the key influencers individually in advance of the meeting to get their committed buy-in, but you'll also want to package your final petition to resonate with the full board. You'll increase the likelihood of securing the desired result if you're explicit about how the additional funds will

- Enable achievement of specific board directives or expand initiatives regarding board priorities (Commanders).

- Permit use of new media such as remote access, DVDs, webinars, blogs, message boards, and virtual meetings (Drifters).

- Ensure increased respect on the Hill for embattled organizational issues and enable a more aggressive posture (Attackers).

- Enable retention of key personnel and alleviate the need to choose sides between large and small members (Pleasers).

- Expand leadership opportunities and intensify media interest (Performers).

- Ensure the survival of the organization and prevent the failure or abandonment of a board-desired outcome (Avoiders).

- Eliminate the drain on reserves and enhance ratios of productivity and organizational health (Analyticals).

To ensure that your message also resonates with Achiever-dominated behavioral styles, be sure to outline how the increased funds will help breathe new life into the mission of the organization.

Of course, tailoring your message so that it appeals to each and every style won't always be necessary, even if multiple styles are present. Often there are only one or two individuals whose positions on an issue will be pivotal. In the nonprofit arena, however, the pivotal decision maker can vary from issue to issue and from venue to venue. Quietly, subtly, but ever vigilant, Achievers don't miss a single raised eyebrow, shift in posture, or acted-out urge to be heard. They're alert to what is said and what isn't said, noticing innuendo and physiology. The Achiever within you is perpetually aware of when the need to adapt is essential and for whom it is essential.

## Actual 360-Degree Input on Achievers

Achievers are nourished and sustained by the positive affects they have on others. Their moment-by-moment awareness of behavioral impacts serves to filter the rough edges from the additional styles resident within their persona. The 360-degree comments about Achievers testify to their ability to awaken the best in others.

### Here's what their superiors have to say:

- *I would never have believed it possible that anyone could inspire such a behavior shift in our problem employee.*

- *Amazing balance of objectivity and empathy.*

- *Never makes excuses, just stands up and takes the hit.*

- *Able to unite a disparate band of rebels into a team.*

- *Took the wounds and resentments that had heaped up in her department over the years and, in assuming her new leadership role, earned esteem from others for her staff.*

- *I rest easy knowing he's got the helm. I trust him, and I'm proud to have him representing us—anywhere, anytime, with anyone.*

## Here's what their peers have to say:

- *I wish I were more like him.*

- *Her example showed me what was indeed possible with talented leadership.*

- *Even though she has moved on, she continues to inspire me daily.*

- *Whenever I face a tough situation, I always think about what he would do.*

- *If it weren't for the inspirational impact of his courage, all of us would have given up.*

- *I didn't earn his help or his trust; instead, I earned the opposite. He could have held a grudge, and frankly, he would have been justified in doing so. But he didn't hesitate to help me at a crucial time in my career. Years later, I'm still in awe of his graciousness.*

## Here's what their subordinates have to say:

- *He stood back, without grimacing, and let me learn.*

- *She understood that I needed understanding.*

- *How did she get that way? Someone, please, teach me!*

- *I'm proud to be on his team.*

- *He made me want to try. I've never really cared about work before—but he made me care.*

- *He believed in me, even when I didn't believe in myself. He took a huge risk in promoting me and that continues to inspire me every single day.*

REMEMBER:
The Achiever resides in all of us.
Although the strengths of the Achiever are at all times available to all of us,
the extent to which we can access those strengths is governed by
our disciplined choice to do so.

# About Your Scores

THE FIRST STEP IN obtaining The Chameleon's Edge is to examine your template of behavioral styles, determining where expanded versatility is needed. You may already have a gut feeling about which behavioral styles are most like you, but it's time now to determine your actual scores and study their implications. Keep in mind that the purpose of the self-assessment is to reveal the degree to which you are most and least like the behavioral styles you've read about. Once you have this information, you're positioned to polish up the rough edges of the behavioral styles you're most like and to build bridges with those whose behavioral styles align with your lower scores. As a reminder from the Preface, here are the seven benefits you'll gain by understanding specifically how to optimize interacting with each of the styles:

- The ability to predict the behavior of others
- Expanded versatility in your own behavioral repertoire
- Increased effectiveness with others
- Perspective that depersonalizes difficult interactions
- A competitive advantage over others whose interpersonal skills are less well developed
- Higher self-esteem
- More control over your vulnerabilities to others

# Three Truths About Behavior Change

Before you undergo the scoring process, recognize that even though you're the one who scored yourself, you may still be uncomfortable with the results. Don't feel alone! Despite the fact that your scores will equip you to develop the versatility needed to increase your success with others, there's no getting around the fact that changes on your part will be required and that those changes will most assuredly cause discomfort. But comfort cannot be the yardstick by which you measure interpersonal success. Indeed, the more you mature the more you realize that it is the very antithesis of comfort that produces interpersonal success. To the extent your scores reveal the need to make some adjustments, these three truths about behavior change may increase your emotional endurance for the growing pains to come.

**Truth 1: The more you need to change your behavior, the less receptive you'll be to doing so.** If you experience a strong sense of resistance to your scores, check in with someone who knows you well. You may have a blind spot. Consider asking that person to score you by downloading additional score sheets at the URL you'll see later in this chapter. Resisting the revelations implicit in your scores and delaying the changes indicated by your scores won't help you. Waiting to develop versatility until the need becomes urgent will only make the process of change exponentially more painful. Don't try to make a 180-degree shift overnight. Integrate one behavior modification at a time and be alert to the results that ensue.

**Truth 2: The more successful you are, the less you feel the need to change your behavior.** It's easy to assume that your success is attributable to your behavior. In fact, for some, success is achieved despite their behavior. More useful than focusing on your current level of success is to ask yourself how much more successful you would be if your behavior were more versatile.

**Truth 3: The more you resist developing versatility, the more you risk not achieving your desired state.** How would you describe your desired state? What are your short- and long-term goals? List all the impediments to achieving these, and consider the extent to which increased versatility would minimize or neutralize the impediments. Study your scores to identify behaviors that are out of alignment with your professional aspirations and be open to making appropriate adjustments so you can move closer to your desired state more quickly.

## Determining Your Scores

You can determine your scores using either of the following two options:

**Option One:** Go to **www.chameleonsedge.com**. Type the ratings you assigned yourself in Figure 2: Self-Assessment Mechanism on page 13 (without changing them!) onto the Self-Assessment on this site. The program will automatically calculate your scores and will produce a printable document at no charge. You'll be able to save your scores in a password-protected account, where they'll be preserved until you retake the test, at which point only your most recent scores will be saved.

**Option Two:** Remove Figure 2, Self-Assessment Mechanism on page 13, and fold vertically along the outer right grid line. Then place it atop the Score Sheet in Figure 4 on page 116 so that the Style Key column is visible. Next, transfer each of your scores into the appropriate spaces in Figure 5, Your Template of Styles, on page 117. For example, "abrupt" is keyed as a Commander trait. If you gave yourself a 2 for this trait, enter that score in the first blank Commander box in Figure 5. You'll have five scores for each behavioral style. Total your scores for each style.

FIGURE 4
# SCORE SHEET

| Characteristic | Style Key |
|---|---|
| ABRUPT | Commander |
| AFRAID OF FAILURE | Avoider |
| ANGRY | Attacker |
| AVOID FINALIZING THINGS | Analytical |
| "BOTTOM LINE" ORIENTED | Commander |
| COMPASSIONATE | Pleaser |
| CONTROLLING | Commander |
| CYNICAL | Attacker |
| DETAIL ORIENTED | Analytical |
| DISORGANIZED | Drifter |
| DOUBLE/TRIPLE CHECK THINGS | Analytical |
| ENJOY SELF | Achiever |
| ENJOY THE SPOTLIGHT | Performer |
| FAST RATE OF SPEECH | Performer |
| FEAR OF RISK | Avoider |
| FLASHY | Performer |
| FREE-SPIRITED | Drifter |
| GROUCHY | Attacker |
| HAPPY | Achiever |
| IMAGINATIVE | Drifter |
| IMPULSIVE | Drifter |
| INTIMIDATING | Attacker |
| JOVIAL | Performer |
| LAID BACK | Drifter |
| NEED EVERYONE TO AGREE | Pleaser |
| PEACEFUL | Achiever |
| PERFECTIONIST | Commander |
| PLEASANT DISPOSITION | Pleaser |
| PRECISE | Analytical |
| "PROCESS" ORIENTED | Analytical |
| REASSURING TO OTHERS | Pleaser |
| RESERVED | Avoider |
| SELF FULFILLED | Achiever |
| PERPETUAL SENSE OF URGENCY | Commander |
| SERENE | Achiever |
| SUBMISSIVE | Pleaser |
| SUPERIOR | Attacker |
| USE LOTS OF CLICHES | Avoider |
| USUALLY IN A HURRY | Performer |
| WORRIER | Avoider |

FIGURE 5
## YOUR TEMPLATE OF STYLES

| Style | Using Figure 4 as the key for Figure 2 (pg. 13), enter your 5 separate scores for each style | | | | | Your Total for Each Style |
|---|---|---|---|---|---|---|
| Commander | | | | | | |
| Drifter | | | | | | |
| Attacker | | | | | | |
| Pleaser | | | | | | |
| Performer | | | | | | |
| Avoider | | | | | | |
| Analytical | | | | | | |
| Achiever | | | | | | |

## Understanding What Your Scores Mean

Your scores delineate, from the highest of 25 to the lowest of 5, the behavioral styles you're most like and least like. Your opportunity is to ensure your Achiever score dominates all your behavioral styles. This will require that you polish up the rough edges of your high scores and build bridges with those who possess your lower scores. Don't make value judgments about the words "high" or "low." High scores aren't necessarily desirable, and low scores aren't necessarily undesirable in the absence of contextual reference.

### High Scores

Ignoring your Achiever score for the moment, find your highest score. This is the behavior you most frequently demonstrate and are most comfortable with.

- Refer to the names and characteristics you identified in the benchmarking exercise A2 on page 11. Do the behaviors you identified in people you find it easy to get along with align with your higher scores? Occasionally, clients discover that their own high score reflects characteristics they identified as belonging to someone they find extremely irritating (from the benchmarking exercise A1 on page 11). This is understandable when you consider that two people can share a trait but deploy it differently, to the chagrin of one another. For example, two Commanders may both be perfectionists, but one imposes this expectation on self only, while the other imposes it on everyone.

- If some of your scores tie, it simply means that you're equally comfortable with and equally as likely to deploy one behavior as the other.

- People tend to validate their own style, believing it to be the best one, the right one. You may even be convinced that you deploy only the best of the characteristics attributed to this style. Remember, no matter what your scores, everyone can use a little polishing up!

- Others whose scores on this style aren't as high as yours don't consider your style to be the best! Your opportunity is to smooth out whatever your rough edges may be. To do this, refer to the relevant chapter and identify which characteristics you need to emphasize and which characteristics you want to de-emphasize.

- If your two highest scores seem to be contradictory (for example, if your Attacker and Pleaser scores are both high), consider whether you're deploying these behaviors in two different venues. Some of us behave quite differently with men than with women, with superiors than with subordinates, and at work versus at home.

- If you struggle to even imagine that anyone wouldn't be able to get along with you, remember that where you score highest, someone else may have the lowest score! That person could someday be your boss, a board member, or a key constituent. If you wait until you must display versatility to develop it, it may be too late.

## Low Scores

Still ignoring your Achiever score, find your lowest score. This is the behavior you find most aggravating and that you most disesteem. You'll find it most challenging to interact effectively with those who manifest behaviors least like your own.

- Recall the names and behaviors of those you identified in A1 on page 11 as being particularly irritating to you. Do their behaviors align with the descriptors of your lower scores?

- Occasionally, clients report that their lowest scores align with a beloved friend, spouse, or other family member or friend. When two people who are devoted to each other have extremely high scores in styles that are in direct opposition (such as Commander and Drifter or Avoider and Performer) you can be sure their Achiever scores are equally high or higher, enabling them to appreciate one another's differences. Although few people succeed in maintaining relationships that personify the old adage that opposites attract, those with high Achiever scores can sometimes pull it off. They rejoice in the balance that each brings to the other and are enhanced by their differences. Deliberately, consciously, and consistently, each plays to the strengths of the other; each shores up the weaknesses of the other; and each is aware of how one augments the other.

- If some of your scores tie, it simply means you are equally disenchanted with and equally likely to be aggravated by these styles.

- There is a natural tendency to validate your dislike for those whose behavior is consistent with your lowest scores. You may even believe those who have this style deserve your disesteem. Remember, everyone, no matter what their scores, has value and utility in the workplace. Others whose scores on this style aren't as low as yours don't consider this style abhorrent. Your opportunity is to become more effective in interacting with this behavior style. To do this, refer back to the relevant chapter and identify packaging techniques you can use to improve interactions with those you believe to have this style.

- If you struggle to imagine making an effort to adapt your behaviors to better work with those who have this style, remember that sooner or later you're going to need to interact successfully with someone whose behavior matches your low score. Learn to do it now, before you're under pressure to do so, before your discomfort with doing so becomes apparent to those who'll be scrutinizing your versatility.

If your scores are consecutive, don't make the mistake of thinking this indicates you get along easily with all behavioral styles. Even consecutive scores can reveal a significant clash when accurately assessed. If your scores are only one or two digits apart, rather than calculating the mathematical difference between your lowest and highest scores, calculate the percent difference between the lowest and highest scores. Here's an example. If your lowest non-Achiever score is 16 and your highest non-Achiever score is 22, the mathematical difference is only 6. Not a big number. However, the percent difference between the two is a significant 37%. ($22 - 16 = 6$; $6 \div 16$ is 37.5%). The discomfort you can anticipate when interacting with those whose behavior is 37% different than your highest score is substantial. The greater the percentage, the greater the need to exercise your versatility and build bridges with those whose behavioral styles align with your lower scores.

Still ignoring your Achiever score, consider whether you disagree strongly with your highest score. If so, worth noting is:

- You scored yourself on both the Self-Assessment Mechanism and on the Predictive Grid. Consider with whom you are in disagreement!
- Don't assume you possess only the negative characteristics of your high score. The higher your Achiever score, the less likely you are to demonstrate the negative traits associated with each style.

## Your Achiever Score

At last it's time to look at your Achiever score!

- Remember, Achievers aren't a discrete style. Everyone has Achiever as part of his or her complement of styles. The more you allow your Achiever to influence and dominate the other styles that make up your repertoire of workplace behaviors, the fewer your rough edges, the easier your interactions with others, and the better your results.
- Recall the names and behaviors of those you identified in benchmarking exercise A3 on page 11 as being particularly inspiring. Do their behaviors align with the descriptors of the Achiever?
- If Achiever is among your highest scores, congratulations! This suggests you're less likely to demonstrate the negative characteristics of your dominant behavioral styles and that you possess the versatility needed to interact successfully with others. But don't get smug! Instead, look for opportunities to deploy the best of your Achiever traits. Inspire difficult others to want to burnish up their own rough edges, and find ways to feature the strengths of others.
- A high Achiever score also indicates that you're adept at diffusing conflict, whether in your own arena or intervening to help others. Achievers have the ability to build bridges among feuding parties to lessen both the duration and the intensity of altercations.
- If your Achiever score is your lowest score, don't despair. Refer to your Self-Assessment Mechanism, noticing that the adjectives keyed to the Achiever are all indicative of the type of relationship you have with yourself. To improve your score, schedule some quality time with yourself, considering whether your chosen profession and your current function aligns with how you're wired and whether you're in a position that features your strengths and minimizes your weaknesses.

## Understanding What Your Scores Don't Mean

Your high scores don't mean that you're forever locked into those particular behavioral styles, and your low scores don't mean that you aren't able to demonstrate those behavioral styles. Indeed, the fundamental premise of this book is that you can develop the versatility to demonstrate any style as needed. However, although the numerical values of your scores can change over time, the relative position of your template of styles isn't likely to change. For example, the intensity of your Attacker and Commander scores may reverse, but if both are currently higher than all other scores, they'll likely remain so. In addition to your own efforts to be more versatile, it is also possible that a different work environment, with different bosses or subordinates, or with the help of a mentor or coach, you may find opportunities to strengthen the positive characteristics and moderate the negative aspects of your dominant styles.

No matter what your template of styles, it doesn't mean you're incapable of adopting or adapting to other styles, but the higher your Achiever score, the easier this is to do. To some extent, you're probably already borrowing selected behaviors from styles that aren't your dominant ones in order to secure specifically desired outcomes. Studying your set of scores will help you identify where and how you might need to expand or intensify such efforts.

Just because you score high in a particular style doesn't necessarily mean you're proficient in the strengths attributed to that style. For example, a high Drifter score doesn't necessarily mean you're a *good* graphic artist or a *good* multimedia director, or a *good* writer. Among the various characteristics of your high scores, you'll need to assess where your real talents lie.

Just because you score low in a particular style doesn't necessarily mean you aren't proficient in the strengths attributed to that style. For example, a high Drifter score doesn't necessarily mean you can't be a good accountant. Perhaps it merely indicates you prefer to apply your fluency with numbers within the venture capital arena. Among the various characteristics of your low scores, you'll need to determine what business context modifications may be necessary to enable your strengths to flourish.

## Predicted Versus Original Scores

As you read about each of the behavioral styles, you were asked to anticipate the degree to which each chapter described your own behavior and to enter a score from 5 to 25 in column B of the Predictive Grid (Figure 3, page 15). In this section, you'll compare the scores on your Predictive Grid to those you assigned yourself before reading about the various behavioral styles. (See Self-Assessment Mechanism on page 13.)

- Enter the totals from "Your Template of Styles" (page 117) into column C of the Predictive Grid.

- Because the scores in column B were entered after you read each chapter, your scoring of yourself in column B reflects your increased knowledge and may be biased toward the characteristics you esteem and against the characteristics you disesteem. The scores in column C came from the Self-Assessment that you completed before reading the book, so they aren't biased by the knowledge you gained in reading about the various styles. Therefore, the more valid of the two columns is C.

- Now compare columns B and C. How closely do your predicted scores in column B align with your original scores in column C? If columns B and C differ by more than 5 points, don't miss the "Ah-Ha's!" For example, if you predicted in column B after reading the book that your Commander score would be 10, and prior to reading the book you assigned a total of 25 points to what you now know is the Commander style, then you're more of a Commander than you realized. If your Commander score in column B is lower than your original scores in column C, perhaps you're less of a Commander than you thought!

- When the score in column C is higher than in column B, it suggests you have greater tendencies toward that style of behavior than you realized. Were you unaware of behavior that is consistent with this score? Under what circumstances or in what venues do you now realize that you're evidencing this behavior?

- When the score in column C is lower than in column B, it suggests you don't have as great a tendency toward that behavior as you anticipated. Could it be that you simply *want* to be more like this style?

- Based on the differences between these two columns, list some specific adjustments you want to make to your behavior and why you think they would benefit you. Come up with at least three steps you will take to improve. Set benchmarks that will indicate that the changes you're making are producing the desired results. Use column D to archive your thoughts.

# A Broader Context for the Prevention and Resolution of Discord

W HETHER FROM WEARINESS, FEAR, or complacency, it can be tempting to lull yourself into ignoring a brewing interpersonal conflict. Although the prospect of confronting the parties involved may be frightening, recognize that, ultimately, the issue will have to be faced, and that you'll pay more dearly the longer you delay. Worth noting is that others' esteem for your maturity increases when you demonstrate the courage to put on the table that which everyone else is trying to ignore. And your own self-confidence is positively affected when you step up and confront conflict. Augmenting the versatility of your newly acquired Chameleon's Edge, a more general discussion of conflict to include both prevention and remedial tactics will be helpful.

## Prevention

Just as the cost of preventive medicine is less than the cost of treatment, it's less taxing to all concerned to prevent destructive discord than to have to remediate it. The following three suggestions equip you to act preemptively when your gut tells you that conflict is brewing.

**Practice early detection.** Informally elicit regular feedback from workplace associates. The idea isn't to pester everyone with seemingly insecure requests for validation. Instead, the opportunity is to demonstrate an ongoing receptivity to input, improvement, and change. Even if you're convinced you have no blind spots, you may be surprised with the answers you get to such questions as the following:

- Can you help me improve in this area?
- What service quality changes would you like to see this quarter?
- What advice do you have for me this year?
- What can I do to help us work even more effectively together?

**Look under the covers.** When you sense that something is wrong, don't let the fact that no explicit complaint has been put forth trump your intuition. Honor your gut feeling while you can still prevent whatever it is from becoming worse. The alternative is to suppress your instincts, wait until the preliminary causal factors fester, and then spend even more time repairing the damage. Here are a few steps that may help you ferret out what underlies your sense of unrest.

- Select a neutral venue to engage relevant others.
- Don't play a guessing game. Be explicit that you sense disharmony.
- Identify vulnerabilities shared by all if the group remains fractured.
- Rather than discussing causal factors, invite solutions only.
- Elicit commitments to the solutions from each participant.

**Back into it.** When your adversary seems more interested in complaining than in solving whatever is amiss between you, this technique is often effective.

- Be explicit about what's at the core of the disagreement.
- Using a medium visible to both of you, such as a white board or flip chart, invite the other party to identify as many ways as possible to inflame or exacerbate the problem.
- Observe that each of the ways to make a situation worse is actually a solution in disguise. Flip each negative statement around to its positive opposite, and you have a group of solution statements.

## Resolution

Whether because you didn't anticipate it or because your efforts to head it off weren't successful, not all conflicts can be prevented. These four techniques can help accelerate the resolution of conflicts already in progress.

**Conduct an excavation.** Knowing what the feuding parties want isn't enough; you must also discern why they want it. To get this information, elicit their continued venting by asking nonjudgmental, curious, and wondering questions. Questions beginning with "why" generate defensiveness. Instead, use open-ended phrases such as:

- Tell me more about…
- And if what you hope for actually occurs, the result you anticipate would be…?
- And this would help you by…?
- So your interest here is to…?

You've succeeded if you've uncovered and are clear about all the reasons that each party wants whatever it is he or she wants.

**Don't leap immediately to solutions.** Even if you can instantly see any number of possible solutions, this isn't the time to articulate them. Instead, take time to empathize with the emotions of others. Don't just regurgitate what was said; acknowledge and honor others' feelings by saying something like:

- Sounds like you're really concerned about…
- So it seems like you're feeling pretty much as if…
- I understand that you're feeling pretty exasperated with…

You've succeeded if the parties confirm your assessment. If more venting occurs at this time, let it happen.

**Elicit acknowledgement of an element of truth in the allegations.** This is crucial because it works to disarm adversaries. If one party self-assesses in a way that's consistent with how their adversary sees them, it'll take a huge amount of wind out of their sails. Examples could include:

- I can see why you think I did that on purpose.
- I can understand why you feel bullied.
- It's clear to me now why you think I've been unfair.
- It must seem to you that I'm making the wrong decision.
- I sure can see why I look like the bad guy right now.

Help the acknowledging party elaborate on these phrases. Be specific about their ability to see their adversary's point of view. You've succeeded if the parties stop trying to affix blame and begin to treat the problem as a shared one.

**Collaboratively vet solutions.** Be prepared to vet more than one solution. Even if you don't identify a mutually agreeable solution, you've been successful if the parties adopt a solution orientation. Think of a few possible solutions and float them for comment. Preface your suggestions with phrases such as:

- What would you think about…?
- How about if we…?
- I wonder if it might help to…?
- Might we consider…?

In most altercations, the one who solves the problem is the one who is committed to constructive forward movement, even when the situation is rife with negativity. It's hard to sustain such a commitment during conflicts, because it means not allowing your behavior to deteriorate in response to the adversarial actions of others. The preventive and remedial techniques described above, when used in conjunction with the essential competence of versatility, will combine to enhance your ability to demonstrate The Chameleon's Edge.

# The Delightful Secret of "The Chameleon's Edge"

THE OPPORTUNITY TO MANIFEST the versatility of The Chameleon's Edge is omnipresent. What constitutes having demonstrated it, however, changes from one circumstance to the next. Endless variables comprise our interactions, making each one unique, so there isn't just one way to achieve or to sustain the "edge" that behavioral versatility brings you. And having it in one instance doesn't guarantee that you'll have it in another.

The only adequately elastic yet accurate depiction of The Chameleon's Edge is as a decision—made scores of times each day, differently each time—to prioritize effectiveness over emotion. Evidencing "the edge" is a deliberate choice to display personal versatility sufficient to optimize your ever-changing interpersonal environment. You'll succeed at doing so every day. And you'll fail at doing so every day. The delightful secret of The Chameleon's Edge is that no matter how many times its advantages have escaped your grasp, you'll have an infinite number of opportunities to try again. In fact, there's another one coming up with your very next interaction!

# Afterword

ABSENT EXTREMELY HIGH ACHIEVER scores, some reporting relationships are particularly acrimonious. Although the use of the adapting techniques presented in this book can take the edge off even the most difficult collaborations, the sustained interaction attendant to reporting relationships puts some behavioral combinations at increased risk of discord. If this describes your situation, consider the following advice:

- Download additional copies of the Self-Assessment Mechanism at www.chameleonsedge.com. Explain that you've already scored yourself, and ask your superior or subordinate to do the same. This will provide a foundation for discussion that is less confrontive and less emotional than would likely occur outside the context of a scoring process.

- Ask that he or she read relevant chapters in this book.

- Each of you identify three specific, valued behaviors that the other is currently demonstrating that have a positive impact toward desired business results.

- Each of you identify three specific behaviors you'd like the other to start or stop doing in furtherance of desired business results.

- Set a date 60 to 90 days out to follow up with each other.

If you're convinced there's no way the other party would ever agree to the above, then go ahead and reveal your own test results, and describe the steps you plan to take to improve the working relationship. This forthright approach usually ushers in a candor that makes possible a substantive discussion about behavior. Such discussions are often all that's needed to stabilize interactions.

# Recommended Reading List

1. *1001 Ways to Reward Employees.* Bob Nelson. Workman Publishing, 1994.

2. *Crucial Confrontations.* Kerry Patterson, Joseph Grenny, Ron McMillan, Al Switzler. McGraw Hill, 2005.

3. *Crucial Conversations.* Kerry Patterson, Joseph Grenny, Ron McMillan, Al Switzler. McGraw Hill, 2002.

4. *Defining Moments.* Joseph L. Badaracco, Jr. Harvard Business School Press, 1997.

5. *Exuberance.* Kay Jamison. Alfred A. Knopf, 2004.

6. *Finding Your Passion.* Cheryl Richardson. Hay House, Inc., 2002.

7. *Good to Great.* Jim Collins.Harper Business, 2001.

8. *It's OK to Be the Boss.* Bruce Tulgan. Harper Collins, 2007.

9. *It's Your Ship: Management Techniques from the Best Damn Ship in the Navy.* D. Michael Abrashoff. Warner Books, 2002.

10. *Nice Girls Don't Get the Corner Office.* Lois P. Frankel. Werner Business Books, 2006.

11. *Powerful Leadership.* E.G. Stephan and R.W. Pace. Prentice Hall, 2002.

12. *Primal Leadership: The Hidden Driver of Great Performance.* Daniel Goleman, Richard Boyatzis, and Annie McKee. Harvard Business School Press, 1991.

13. *Smart Questions.* Dorothy Leeds. Jossey-Bass, 2004.

14. *The 21 Irrefutable Laws of Leadership Tested by Time.* J.L. Garlow. Nelson Publishers, 2002.

15. *The Leadership Challenge.* James M. Kouzes and Barry Z. Posner. Jossey-Bass, 2002.

16. *The No Asshole Rule.* Robert I. Sutton. Werner Business Books, 2007.

17. *The Oz Principle.* Roger Connors, Tom Smith and Craig Hickman. Prentice Hall Press, 1994.

18. *The World's Most Powerful Leadership Principle.* James C. Hunter. Crown Business, 2004.

19. *Working With You is Killing Me.* Katherine Crowley and Kathi Elster. Werner Business Books, 2006.

20. *What Winners Do to Win.* Nicki Joy. Wiley and Sons, Inc., 2003.

21. *Six Thinking Hats.* Edward de Bono. Back Bay Books, 1985.

22. *Hiring and Keeping the Best People.* Harvard Business School Press, 2002

23. *Influence Without Authority.* Allan R. Cohen and David L. Bradford. John Wiley and Sons, Inc., 2005.

24. *A Briefing for Leaders.* Robert L. Dilenschneider. Harper Business, 1992.

25. *Beyond the Wall of Resistance.* Rick Maurer. Bard Press, 1996.

26. *Taking Advice.* Dan Ciampa. Harvard Business School Press, 2006.

27. *Leading Through Conflict.* Mark Gerzon. Harvard Business School Press, 2006.

28. *Courage.* Gus Lee. Jossey-Bass, 2006.

29. *True Professionalism.* David H. Maister. Simon and Shuster, 1997.

30. *The DNA of Leadership.* Judith E. Glaser. Platinum Press, 2006.

31. *How to Become an Employer of Choice.* Roger E. Herman and Joyce L. Gioia. Oakhill Press, 2000.

# Bibliography

"2020 Vision: The Future of Work" by Penna Publishers 2003.

"Economic Development Reference Guide" by International Economic Development Council, 2006.

"Impending Crisis: What's Coming…What to Do." Roger E. Herman. The Herman Group, 2004.

"Integrating Telework, Flextime and Officing for Work Force 2020." John S. Niles. Global Telematics, commissioned by Hudson Institute Center for Workforce Development, January 1999.

"Preventing the 2010 Meltdown." Edward E. Gordon. Imperial Corp., 2005.

"Red Alert, 2005 Employment Advisory." Roger E. Herman. The Herman Group, Inc., July 2005.

"Red Alert, 2006 Employment Advisory." Roger E. Herman. The Herman Group, Inc., July 2005.

"SHRM 2004-205 Workplace Forecast: A Strategic Outlook." Society of Human Resource Management, June 2004.

"SHRM Human Capital Benchmarking Study: 2006 Executive Summary." Society of Human Resource Management, June 2006.

"The Future." www.aaai.org/AITopics/html/future.html, Association for the Advancement of Artificial Intelligence, 2006.

"The Network News." Sloan Work and Family Research Network. Boston College, February 2005.

"The Next 20 Years." Jacqueline Emigh. TNTY (The Next Twenty Years) E-Newsletter, July 15, 1998.

"Work/Life Balance Takes Priority." www.spherion.com, 2003.

"Workforce 2020." TalentSmart, 2003.

# About the Author

FRANCIE DALTON specializes in the communication, behavioral, and management sciences. Her firm, Dalton Alliances, Inc., is a premier business consultancy enabling management to meet critical objectives in leadership development, metrics-based performance, team building, recruitment, and retention. Among her offerings are fully customized assessments such as 360's; member and employee surveys; and an array of follow-up services including developmental workshops, interventions, and executive coaching.

Dalton's work in the area of leadership development has been featured in *Harvard Management Update, CEO Magazine, Investor's Business Daily, American Way Magazine, The New York Post, MSN Money, The New York Times,* and more. She has been a regular columnist for the *Washington Business Journal* on issues of leadership, and has appeared on CNN Financial News Network, where she was interviewed about her work in the areas of leadership and performance measures.

A veteran of the Vietnam Era, Dalton was trained as a German linguist, spending four and one-half years with the U.S. Army Military Intelligence Service. She then took her master's degree in business from Johns Hopkins University and founded her firm in 1991. Adjunct faculty at the University of Maryland, Francie taught business management to doctoral candidates from 1994 to 2003. With dozens of published works to her credit, she is a frequent speaker in the nonprofit sector whose clients include scores of CEOs and senior executives throughout the United States.

Her email address is fmdalton@daltonalliances.com; the Dalton Alliances, Inc., website is www.daltonalliances.com.

# Other Published Works by Francie Dalton

"Succeeding a Legend," *Associations Now,* August 2008.

"Poisonous Passivity," *Corporate Incentive Travel,* June 2008.

"Botox for Problem Solving," *Transaction World,* April 2008.

"Justify Inaction," *The Enterprise,* October 2007.

"Motivating the Unmotivated," A White Paper published by *The Journal of Compensation and Benefits,* July/August 2007.

"Retention," *Forum,* June 2007.

"Decisions on Demand," *The Nova Scotia Business Journal,* June 2007.

"Motivating the Unmotivated," *The Merchant Magazine,* May 2007.

"Playing Deaf Dumb and Blind to the Complaints About Your Hires," *The Minority Women in Business,* April 2007.

"Are You Ready to Assess Your Success?" *The Fluid Power Journal,* January/February 2007.

"Coaching Your CEO Toward Improved Delegation," *Alaska Business Monthly,* November 2006.

"Neutralizing the Toxic Dumper," *Credit Union Management,* October 2006.

"CEO's Assistant and Evil Witch?" *The Business Journal,* September 2006.

"Pivotal Decisions," *Associations Now,* July 2006.

"Neutralize Toxic Dumpers Who Kill Work's Atmosphere," *Washington Business Journal,* June 2006.

"Excuses to Do Nothing are Usually Just No Good," *Washington Business Journal,* August 2006.

"A COO to Run the Show?" *Washington Business Journal,* June 2006.

"When Executive Assistants Trade in Resistance, Drama," *Washington Business Journal,* June 2006.

"Exposing the Inexcusable Excuses for Not Handling Conflict," *Promotional Business Products,* June 2006.

"Excuses, Excuses, Excuses," *Business Credit,* April 2006.

"Scrutiny May Hurt but Yields Results," *Facilities Engineering Management,* March 2006.

"Forgo Egos, Hire CEOs With Substance," *Washington Business Journal,* January 2006.

"Emotions in Motion Throw off Judgment," *Washington Business Journal,* January 2006.

"Five for Fighting," *Washington Business Journal,* December 2005.

"Can You Handle Your Own Truth?" *Washington Business Journal,* November 2005.

"That's Truly Frightening: Execs Who Fear Technology," *Washington Business Journal,* October 2005.

"Does Delegating Divide Staff, but Conquer No Goal?" *Washington Business Journal,* September 2005.

"Working Successfully with the Seven Workplace Behavioral Types," published in the American Management Association, "Mworld," Summer/Fall 2005.

"Using 360 Degree Feedback Mechanisms," published in "Occupational Health & Safety," July 2005.

"Metrics Based Management," *The Journal Of Association Leadership,* Summer 2005.

"Driven to Leadership, What is the Right Track for You?" *Washington Business Journal*, March 2005.

"Harness the Power and Utility of 360 Degree Feedback," *Partner Advantage*, February 2005.

"Delegation Pitfalls," *Association Management*, February 2005.

"Don't Ignore Gut Instincts, Just Don't Call 'Em That," *Washington Business Journal*, February 2005.

"Clear Evidence: Stand Out by Pointing to Outcomes," *Washington Business Journal*, December 2004.

"So You Wanna be a COO?" *Biz Life*, October 2004.

"Evidence Based Performance Measures," *Business Update*, January 2004.

"Hire When Ready," *Association Management*, July 2003.

"Constructive Change Comes From Within," *Association Management*, September 2002.

"The Eight Classic Types of Workplace Behavior," *HR Magazine*, September 2000.

## Learn More About Versatility

Here are four additional resources to help you extend the educational experience of *Versatility*.

1. Consider bringing "The Chameleon's Edge" workshop to your organization. This is a one- or two-day session tailored to the specific needs of your group. Augmented by workbooks and a competitive review session, this delightfully funny, fast-paced, introspective, and highly substantive seminar promises to help your employees increase their versatility.

2. Contribute to the repository of case studies that exemplify the behavioral styles you've read about. Tell us your stories about workplace interactions, and read the stories of others. Share lessons learned, and participate in live "Question and Answer" sessions. Gain access to all this and more by visiting **www.franciesmessageboard.com**.

3. Visit **www.chameleonsedge.com** for additional resources, including

   • a white paper about how to reward each behavior style when additional compensation isn't available

   • a compilation of provocative review questions to stimulate group discussion

   • a laminated card summarizing key points for each style

4. Consider the utility of helping your board, volunteers, committees, and members increase their versatility. This topic is a popular choice for convention plenary and breakout sessions. Contact Francie Dalton directly at francie@daltonalliances.com or by calling 1-800-442-3603.